A Desire to *Belong*

Journey into Self-Discovery

By Steven Kearney Sims

XULON PRESS

Xulon Press
2301 Lucien Way #415
Maitland, FL 32751
407.339.4217
www.xulonpress.com

Paperback ISBN-13: 978-1-66283-653-4
Ebook ISBN-13: 978-1-66283-654-1

A Desire to *Belong*

Journey into Self-Discovery

Acknowledgement

A Desire to Belong originally published in 2005 was the very first book I'd ever written. For quite a while I've had the desire to write a revised version. During the writing of the orginal once realizing the book was really happening I allowed my lack of patience to override God's timing. The thought of me of all people as a published author was overwhelming to say the least. After publication I knew I had made a mistake by moving ahead of myself and God leaving me unsatisfied. I'd forgotten who the true author was, who had brought me to this place and time.

With never a thought or plan of writing anything I knew this book wasn't my idea because suddenly felt the need to share my story. Unknowledgeable of the whole writing and publishing process I really had no idea what I was doing. As the pages began to accumulate reflecting the part of me which had been forced down and buried under the self- created mess I began to see my work as a part of God's continuing healing process releasing the past that had held me bound for years.

Physically and verbally abused as a child led me to a self-destructive lifestyle lasting thirty plus years. Always believing my upbringing had stripped me of the person I was meant to be I became content with the person I had become, a person I came to think very little of. However deep down I always felt I was better than the person I had become, I just didn't know how to reach that person. Each time I attempted to reconstruct my life I was met by failure leading right back where I was.

Tired of living an empty existence and finally reaching the end of my rope I cried out to God while attempting to end my life. I cried like a baby to awake only to find I was met by failure once again. Shortly afterwards things went from bad to worse and when I thought I'd reached a dead end out of options I called on the only one that might hear me if he truly existed. Suddenly questions began to be answered, direction began to be given and all I had to do was be willing to follow. As I continued following changes began to take place in me and since that time life has never been the same.

I would have never believed that an invisible God could impact and transform a person had I not experienced it firsthand. It truly was and is an amazing experience and journey I'll never forget. A journey that had to be shared. Thank you Father for another chance.

A Desire To Belong

As we grow going through life's experiences we come to realize the existence of good and bad. In time it eventually leads us to the larger question of the existence of God and Satan, heaven and hell. Unfortunately there's never been any undisputable evidence among humanity, there's only what we as individuals choose to believe. So the next question points toward those who choose to believe, where does that belief come from? Is it from word of mouth? Is it from a book which if allowed could produce a blind faith? Could it actually be from some unexplainable as well as unforgettable experience that has taken place in that person's life?

The first advice given to anyone concerning writing is making sure it's a topic you know about, I figure who knows more about me than me. Therefore I hold wholeheartedly to my belief of the existence of God, of a heaven and hell but it's not a belief I always had. Raised in Passaic, NJ in a household where I never felt I belonged my biological mother falling on hard times gave me up at the age of two to an older couple who owned their own home with the belief

1

they would be able to provide a more stable and fulfilling life for me than she was able to.

Previously socially knowing them because of their living status believed them to be good people. Also noticing they had no kids in the home she believed would make a perfect fit but for me it turned out to be anything but. Both of my adopted patents were born in the south during the early 1900s. I once heard my adopted father say he was born in 1910, being curious I calculated how old he was when I entered into their life. He was forty-eight so my adopted mother was about forty-five, at two years old both were old enough to be my grandparents.

Growing up in the south during a time when needing all hands working towards the welfare of the family neither had the privilege of attending school therefore neither were real big on education. It was a time when kids were seen but not heard, a time where you were only told something once, a time when a belt did most of the talking. Although it was now the mid-1900s I grew up in the traditions of the early 1900s.

A Desire To Belong

The man of the house was a hardworking man who worked the same job close to forty years. He was a good provider for his family and from what I knew a man with of strong faith in God. A dedicated member and deacon in the church we attended he rarely missed a church service which led my adopted mother to follow. In spite of my overall feelings although far from perfect I must say he was a decent man. On the other hand my adopted mother, a stay at home wife was a mean spirited person who seemed to be unsatisfied unless there was drama in the air. Unless you stayed in agreement with her opinions whether family or friend, in her mind you was now the enemy until she decided otherwise. Her disposition was like that of a ticking time bomb, never knowing when or what would set her off, and where I was concerned it didn't take much.

It seemed as if she only had to look in my direction and the fireworks would begin. Each day was like walking on eggshells trying not to make a sound not wanting to be noticed, just trying to get through each day without feeling her wrath. I remember times when my father would come in from work and for whatever reason disagreements would arise. The yelling would start sometimes even getting physical but never out of hand mainly because my mother would run and lock herself in the bathroom for a time. During those times I would always find myself in a dark area of the house crying while asking God for help, for protection. My fear wasn't just for that period of time but I knew that because my mother couldn't satisfy her anger directed towards my father it would be reflected onto me the following day.

Going to church as a family I heard the preaching of a God who created all things, who sees and knows all things and who was a Savior for all. However I couldn't see how that applied to me because my life was a living hell. I was convinced that if there was a God he didn't care about me or even knew I existed. By ten years old verbally and physically abused on a daily bases I came to believe there was something wrong with me. According to the information I was constantly fed I was as stupid as the days are long. I was no good just like my no-good birth mother and would never be any good.

That's why she gave me away, she knew something was wrong with me. She'd continue telling how she didn't want me either but they, referring to my biological mother and a friend who later took on the title of godfather begged her to take me in. I remember meeting my biological mother I thought for the first time when I was about eight years old. Learning later in life I had spent my first two years with her in my mind it was as if those years never existed. From as far back as I can remember until I was about eight my adopted parents would host an after-hours joint in our basement on weekends. I looked forward to Friday and Saturday nights. We were the last house of a dead end street and on weekends starting about 11pm cars would start pulling in and lining up until the dead end looked like a parking lot.

Being on a dead end street I guess it was a perfect after hour hideaway. Most times I'd be upstairs in my bed listening to traffic as they pile in. Between four and five in the morning they would start making their way elsewhere. Our basement was small and had a low ceiling but supplied enough room for a build-in bar with a few barstools and a decent sized lodge area. Behind the bar displayed bar paraphernalia along with the different brands of hard liquors. My father would tend bar while my mother would prepare and sell fried chicken with homemade biscuits made from scratch. These biscuits unlike her were heavenly. Usually I would be upstairs in bed listening as the people arrived through the front door but this particular night I was up watching TV.

A lady younger than my adopted had come up from the basement and her and my mother were talking. All of a sudden my adopted mother called me over while the lady was standing there, she asked me if I knew who she was. With my head down after quickly looking up giving a glance and said no. She said, this is your birth mother and left it there. Dumbfounded I just stood there not knowing what to do or say. Then she asked, ain't you gonna say hi?

I spoke then she spoke and asked how I was doing and from there I was sent to bed and it was never spoke of again.

I also had a bad stuttering problem and the more nervous I became the worse my stuttering became and I was nervous most of the time. Whenever I'd try to respond to my adopted mother I would barely be able get a word out and she would become so angered she'd began yelling and cursing me out. I recall the time while fortunate enough to be out in front of the house playing she called me in. She noticed I wasn't stuttering as much out with the other kids as I did when around her and asked why, when I couldn't answer without stuttering she drew back and slapped me across the face. She said something else I can't recall then sent me back outside. This was my life.

Numerous times I found myself asking God why he created me the way he did, an unlovable misfit. Why did he even create me at all? Why, Why God? At eight years of age I was wishing I had never been born. How does a child's mind even began to process such thoughts and emotions? It was also around this time when they adopted another child. I recall a woman dressed in a nurse's uniform showing up at our front door holding a baby, she soon departed but the one year old baby girl remained.

Rhonda became my father's pride and joy, the only girl, the one who couldn't do any wrong. As she grew whenever my mother tried to discipline her my adopted father would step up in her defense but never once stepped up in mine, if anything joined in. I don't recall who told me but someone shared my father once suggested to my mother she try talking to me instead of always beating on me and she responded talking won't do any good and so I guess that was that.

I now felt even more of an outsider. My adopted mother hadn't failed to stressed daily how much wish she had never laid eyes on me and even though I not only heard but felt it daily now that feeling was intensified by the double standards I was witnessing. Rhonda definitely was no angel by a long short, I remember a lot of yelling but not one beating because my father won't allow it. Another thing my adopted mother was good for was using us in comparison. During her episodes she would ask, why you can't be like your brother Leroy, he never gave us any trouble, which I later found to be a lie.

Leroy was their first adopted child, fifteen years older than me he was long gone before I entered the picture. However when I got older Leroy and I would compare notes of our childhoods and he swears till this day he had it worse than I but mainly by the hands of our adopted father. He also shared he ran away from home numerous times and had to go to court but unlike me he was unfearful telling the judge what was going on and the judge was able to put an end to his physical abuse. Now her comparison methods shifted towards Rhonda asking why you can't be like your sister, she don't give us any trouble.

Because of my mother I began having ill feeling towards Rhonda but she didn't make it any easier either. She became my mother's little spy telling Rhonda if she ever seen me doing or saying something I shouldn't report it back to her and Rhonda seemed more than happy to. I actually believe she enjoyed getting me in trouble. I had just turned sixteen when I was allowed to go to my first music concert with a friend who lived a few houses away. Because the friend had asked my mother she agreed however the deal to me was I couldn't go unless I took Rhonda with us to ensure I came straight back home when it was over, an eight year old as my chaperone.

During that evening out I slipped up and said a curse work and Rhonda heard it, the next thing I heard was ouuuu, I'm gonna tell mommy. When we got home she couldn't wait to tell. My mother even wanted to know what the word was I guess to see what punishment it warranted. If I recall correctly I got slapped and put on punishment. Rhonda was also picking up so of our adopted mother's characteristics. I remember her inviting friends to the house and then all of a sudden she was throwing them out while telling them not to ever come back. The deck was undoubtedly stacked against me,

I couldn't win for losing. Jumping ahead just for a minute, even as I grew older and could no longer be restricted to the house sometimes coming in and out I would have a friend with me and they would act so well-mannered in front of her days later she'd start, why can't you be like so-n-so.

Most of them she'd only seen a couple time for seconds but because of the impression they left she only seen what she wanted to see. Little did she know they were heroin users, alcoholics and more but she always seen me as less than. Back on track, by age ten I was running away from home on a regular but with nowhere to go, no one to turn to within days I would just allow myself to be picked up by my parents who'd been riding around looking for me. I already knew what the outcome would be, only to end up right back where I had no desire to be. Most of my decisions to run away was during school. For me school was like being on furlough from hell.

It was my opportunity to leave the fear, hostility and confusion behind for those hours. Besides the fact that I already had a beating waiting for me once I got home which you'll find out the reason shortly, school also had rules and when those rules were broken consequences followed. With low self-esteem and short attention span I found it hard keeping a constant focus on my schoolwork. Children are not designed to deal with stressful environments or situations therefore children can't learn well if they're not emotionally well. Away from home the last thing on my mind was work, any kind of work. All I wanted to do was relax my mind from the haunting and stressful existence that was my reality.

Sometimes my decision to run away from hone would be made after exhausting my warnings ending with the school principle calling my house informing my mother of the misbehavior with a request that a parent appear for a face to face conference. Knowing the outcome at the end of that day while everyone else was happily heading home, home was the last place I wanted to go. It was also one of the few times my father would take full interest. When a parent was requested in our house although my mother was home all day it was always my father who appeared.

Angered for having to take off from work I knew what that meant once he got home. They both followed the same routine, strip, forced to lay across the bed on my stomach and beat with a leather belt. I was already feeling an enormous weight, imagine not being able to remember a day of your childhood when you didn't get a beating.

I became a constant bed wetter and as a constant remedy my adopted mother believed she could beat it out of me with a leather belt while forced to lie across the bed unclothed face down. Sometimes she talked as if she believed I was just too lazy to get up and go to the bathroom. Even as a child that notion made no sense to me. Why would anyone in his or her right mind choose to do that? Put aside the consequences I faced daily, it was very uncomfortable night after night having to lay in my own urine half the night and to think I'd do it on purpose was madness.

No matter how hard I tried, how much I didn't want to it continuously happened, and I got beat for it every time. She would make it her business to check my bed every morning and all day while in school my mind reflected what was waiting for me once I got home. All I was constantly hearing was how sorry she was to have ever laid eyes on me I just didn't want to go back. She didn't want me there anyway so I felt everyone was better off if I didn't.

For days I would find myself running the streets during the day and sleeping in basements, garages, unlocked cars on car lots, wherever I found comfort and warmth, and I felt at ease. I remember one day she asked me why I kept running away and after repeating her words back to her she called me stupid for believing what she said and claimed it was my fault, I made her respond that way. Then she asked, you know I love you right? In my mind to disagree was not a smart thing to do so I felt I had no choice but to agree, but it didn't change anything.

Running away became so frequent by thirteen like Leroy I found myself standing in front of a judge for the first time in my life. With my parents standing beside me and very little trust in authority figures when required to speak I would literally shut down. My nerves would become so rattled making my stuttering even worse it was almost impossible to get one word out. Therefore I'd become accustom to responding with the only three words I never had a problem getting out "I don't know" which in my mother's case only added gasoline to the fire.

The judge ask me why I kept running away, I don't know was my response, the next question was if I wanted to go back home with them but unlike Leroy I was afraid to say what I really wanted to so my response with yes. You may still ask why? In my mind who listened to kids over grownups, what if I said no and he sent me back anyway, the least of my problems would be never hearing the end of it. As if things weren't bad enough, every time my adopted mother would have looked in my direction remembering that day life would be practically unbearable. I can hear it now, all we've done for you, took you in when your birth mother didn't ever want you. We put a roof over your head, feed and put clothes your sorry ass and you don't want to be here. Things were bad enough, I'd only be adding fuel to the fire.

I was maybe ten years old and another heartfelt phrase I'd constantly hear was how the devil was in me causing me to act a fool. I had heard it so much that once during her lashing out she asked why I acted so stupid and I answered, because the devil was in me, I shouldn't have said that. She hit the roof, the devil's in you ah, well I'm gonna beat that devil out of you. I can't remember what happened next because so much has been blocked out for so long those memories can no longer be accessed.

There is one very special memory I will never forget which was shocking but well needed. Being told by my adopted mother years earlier I knew I was adopted. I was thirteen still in my runaway child stage when I met a biological sister I never knew I had which started a chain reaction of wonder. However the way I met her is a different story. My belief is my biological mother contacted my adopted mother giving her the news and practically begged her to take me to see my sister believing she only had a short time left to live.

In any case my adopted mother got the new of after being stabbed my sister was in the hospital in ICU. She told me where we were going, who we were going to see and even told me she wasn't expecting to live much longer. Reaching the hospital room a little shaken not knowing what to expect she went ahead. Moments later she motioned me forward, I walked up to the bed where my sister Connie laid smiling at me with tubes seemingly coming from everywhere.

I was amazed to see how much she looked like me or since she was older I looked like her. We said a few words and I felt a connection right away as I'm sure she did because she knew and remembered me as a baby. She did live about a year past our reunion and hoping my adopted mother never found out I spent as much time with her as possible. An even bigger surprise was Connie was living with an older sister Helena so now I had two sisters. They may not have known because by their early passing the relationship was to short lived, but in the time we did share together they became my pride and joy.

I even went as far as to sneak and pack a suitcase, dropped it out the second floor window, snuck downstairs and out the front door planning to run away and move in with them but that didn't work. For one thing Helena also had two young children, my niece and nephew who also lived in the four room apartment and that was enough reason. But I was also a juvenile runaway and that could bring legal problems nobody wanted. Soon I would began visiting and getting to know my biological mother and three younger brothers Howard, Eddie, and Lawrence I never knew I had.

Although I didn't grow up around my biological family there was no denying that any of us were her biological children because we all had such a strong resemblance to her. My niece and mother before her passing not long ago at ninety-four would call me her twin. I can see even clearer now that was one of if not the main judgement my adopted mother had against me. Thinking back at all the times I'd hear how much she wished she'd never laid eyes on me plus personally knowing my biological mother, seeing how much I looked like her I believe at first she really didn't want me because of the strong resemblance.

She'd also highlight how my so-called god-father and biological mother begged her to take me. I believe when she looked at me she really didn't see me, she seen her and my adopted mother didn't know how to handle it, so I'd end up feeling and wearing her frustration. I'd frequently hear in a screaming voice how much I looked like my biological mother and how I'd turn out to be no good just like her.

I still remember moments of stealing away in the darkness crying while repeatedly asking God to rescue me from this painful existence but there never seemed to be any response. And if things weren't bad enough I found myself also paying for my adopted fathers transgressions. There were times in the evenings when he'd come in from work.

We'd all sit and have dinner together and afterwards I'd leave the kitchen and that's when the conversation would began. I would hear her from the next room accusing him of having an affair.

Sometimes it would become so heated I would hear my mother run into the bathroom off from the kitchen and lock the door behind her. I knew the door was locked because I'd hear him yelling for her to open up. It never went much further than that. However, we hear talk of a woman's scorn, I think my adopted mother was the originator. As I shared earlier, she was a mean spirited person who held grudges, the type of person who looked to get even.

Whenever these episodes would occur I knew there would be hell to pay the following day. She wasn't able to get even with him so the following days she'd take her frustration out on me. I would be attacked at every turn because nothing I'd do was right. If there was a heaven and hell I was already in one of them. Through regular weekly church services I came to believe in someone or something greater than ourselves but through my experience he only existed as judge over our actions and made the final decision whether we entered heaven or hell, other than that as far as I could see, I was on my own.

There's a saying which goes birds of a feather flock together. By the time I'd reached mid-teens I found myself drawn to other teens as troubled as myself. With such a low opinion of myself I felt I had no identity of my own. I began to follow the characteristics of others. These were young teens who were constantly in and out of youth detention centers eventually ending up in prisons. However there was something different about me. What I possessed within which most of them lacked was a belief in someone or something greater than ourselves.

My belief produced boundaries in my life, in other words there were limits to my madness which they lacked. However existing out of my element was stretching those boundaries. I also knew guys as well that never got into trouble but to me there was no life, no excitement and I craved excitement. Only able to see where I'd been I felt I'd been caged up most of my life and I had a lot to make up for. Based on my limited experience I believed good guys always got looked or walked over therefore I no longer wanted to be that good guy.

That's how I ended up out of my element, trying to escape myself, wanting to re-invent myself. Although unaware at the time God had heard my many silent pleas for protection and it came to pass only not in my time but His, when it really became life threatening. Looking back over those years when believing He had no concern for me, today I know better. I've followed the same paths as many that I've witnessed fallen prey to self-destruction but because I managed to avoid the same fate, I don't fool myself to believing I was any better than they were. Today I know the hand of God was on my life through the seed planted in me years earlier of someone greater than ourselves.

Today with a stronger belief and knowledge of God as I review the past realizing I had to endure many heartaches, through it all I was learning valuable lessons that would benefit me even to this day. I often think of how my life could have turned out without the boundaries produced by a belief of a higher power. Later in life I would suffer incarceration but never for felonies that required prison time. Reluctantly I have to give my adopted mother some credit for not allowing me to run as I desired because I can see now how easy it would have been reaching that point of no return.

Most who I chose to follow did eventually end up doing prison time, some even dying while incarcerated, I could have easily been in that number. Through the constant cruelness that plagued my existence positive qualities also emerged. From my adopted mother I learned to be self-efficient always feeling like I stood alone in the world. No one truly cared so there was no one I could depend on. Secondly she showed me the type of person I didn't want to be, the mean-spirited person that she was. She was the type of person you'd rather avoid if necessary.

To prove my point although I was very young I recall three to four weeks during the summer months my aunts would send their kids to our house as a vacation for both parties, themselves and the kids. A custom before my arrival, a certain time during the summer kids would suddenly show up and although I was relieved to have others in the house it didn't change the circumstances. From Baltimore there was Preacher who talked a lot of nonsense and loved big girls and fried chicken, I guess that's how he got that nickname.

His not identical twin sister Wilma was more on the quite side and loved spending her time rocking. Give her a rocking chair and she'd be in rocking heaven. However she didn't necessarily need a chair that rocks to get her rocking on, any couch or regular wood chair would do just as good. Then there was their older brother Nick who was the character always looking for something, not always legal to get into.

Not a bad looking fella at about 5'8 and slim build he also saw himself as a lady's man and from what I remember he didn't do half bad. I still remember one female he brought up with him from Baltimore. I was about thirteen years old, she was about his height, caramel color skin with medium brown hair. Every time he brought her around when I looked at her my heart would flutter, and when she smiled at me I felt like I might faint, but I never did.

Their father in his early fifties had long remarried but you couldn't tell because every weekend you could find him out driving his 1975 mid-green Cattie with yellow skirts making his rounds while chasing females half his age. For those who don't know skirts were made to attach across the rear wheel portion of the fender covering the top portion of the tire. He was also about 5'8, light skin, thin and loved attention and Nick was truly his father's son.

Carol Lee, my adopted mother's deceased brother's daughter was from Arkansas, a tall light skin sister resembling Angela Davis, a mid-sixties and seventies black activist who was on the run accused of killing a law enforcement officer.

I remember them being out and arriving back at the house talking about being stopped by the cops thinking she was Angela Davis. Thank God they didn't shoot first and then decide to ask questions. Then there was Michelle, my mother's sister's granddaughter who lived in the projects on the other side of town. Michelle had the looks to qualify for supermodel status but raised in the projects where old and young predators lurk, raised by a young single mother still not fully committed to motherhood working a full time job the odds were not good.

Years later all of us grown and coming together including Leroy who was the oldest of us all, they'd laugh about me being the youngest and how they would tease and even terrorize me just for fun. After writing this I'm trying to imagine the thoughts they may have had first seeing me. Even in the midst of a full house I was still alone. I can remember getting beat for things they'd done and blamed me for, and because of my fear and stuttering I was unable to verbally defend myself. I remember I was about seven or eight when my mother had a caged bird.

This particular Saturday my parents had gone food shopping leaving the cousins and myself at the house. For some reason Preacher opened the cage and the bird got out. Now everyone's running around frantic trying to catch the bird and it lands in the kitchen sink. Preacher turns the water on full blast and kills the bird. When my parents returned they all got together and said I opened the cage and killed the bird. There was no question a beating would follow. One thing they really got a kick out of was telling the stories of when I was a baby how they would always let Preacher carry me and he'd always drop me.

The fact that I always land on my head yelling and screaming was hilarious to them. They all seen my hardship as a joke but I managed to laugh along with then as big boys should. However my main reason for bringing up these family members is that when they all got older and came into town to visit they would show up at every family member's house except ours.

I would have to go to other family member's houses to see them. I guess it wasn't much of vacation for them after all. Leroy lived less than two blocks away for a time and rarely visited. That says a lot of the type of impact she left on us all. She would hear they were in town visiting and get highly upset and hurt because none of them who she played a part in their lives when they were kids ever stopped by to visit her but as it's written, we reap what we sow. There was no difference when I moved out, it would be months, maybe a year or more between visits.

I still recall clearly years ago during a visit looking at family photos and noticing there was not one photograph of me smiling but always a sad empty look. Honestly I can't remember anything happy memories growing up in that house. Not having much of a childhood most of my time was spent cleaning while being tormented. Today I do the cleaning in our home because it's instilled in me. I can clean better than most women including my wife.

I never cooked while growing up but stuck in the house quite often I absorbed enough to also find my way around the kitchen pretty well. The one good thing talked about by many family and friends was my mother's cooking skills which was outstanding. I'm talking old school down home southern cooking when everything was made from scratch without ever having to use a measuring cup. When I finally moved out on my own I found that I had no problem living alone.

I was able to cook and clean better than most females and I took pride in that. There are times I think back at my mother's temperament because no one is born mean-spirited so what happened in her life to make her that way? No one truly knows but her and God. I have my own ideas by the information I received later in life. She once had a biological son who died from unnatural circumstances while under the care of a babysitter. Never having another child of her own by my own observation I believe she carried a blame she was never able to forgive herself for which turned to bitterness.

When you're able to love yourself how can you love others? They also make it hard for others to love them. My adopted father wasn't much of a dad in the home.

As an adult I learned more about him from others after his passing than I knew when he was alive and what I was hearing made me wish I would have known that person. He worked long hours and mostly in and out of the house. When I rose for school he was off to work returning in the evenings in time for dinner and shortly afterwards retiring to bed to repeat the process. However as I said he was a man of faith who prayed on a regular bases.

In fact many in the church referred to him as the praying deacon because his prayers could last fifteen minutes or more easily. The one thing I remember well is that he rarely if at all missed a night on his knees praying before getting into bed. A few years after his passing a fellow deacon of his and I were talking and he shared something my father had shared with him, "referring to me he said, you see that boy over there, I hope he turns out to be some-body". I know he wasn't always in agreement with the treatment I was receiving but he never intervened.

The one thing I'm sure of is that in has many prayers he prayed for me, and I believe those prayers helped sustain me over the years to come. He wasn't much for doing around the house but he was a great provider for his family. He provided home security and my mother handled of the rest. I learned by his example about good work ethics and responsibility although later in life I held to one and ran from the other but both remained instilled in me. Dropping out of school at sixteen it was made clear to me there would be no lounging around the house.

I had to get a job and pay my parents rent which was thirty-five dollars a week, and if I missed a week I had to make it up the following week. The lesson was a landlord don't want to hear sad stories and neither did they. Needless to say I wasn't happy with the arrangement in the least but it taught me the valuable truth that nothing is given free of charge. However, I believe even through the harsh treatment their most valuable lesson received was that of respect for others as well as myself.

Living this life I've learned genuine respect will prompt a genuine response and it will take you a greater distance in life. I'm sure you've noticed how most times I refer to her as my adopted mother and that's because my childhood was spent terrified of a person I should have been able to love and respect. Now I refer to her as Cora which was her name. I had to learn to forgive and let go in order to move on but I can never forget unless I get Alzheimer's.

The main thing my childhood taught me to be was insecure. I wish I could say I loved her or even respected her because even that could have been generated by fear. ***Romans 8:28 of the bible tells us that <u>God causes all things</u> to work together for good to those who love God, those who are called according to His purpose***. I can't even say I liked God back then because all I'd witnessed was disappointment. I could have easily dismissed the belief of His existence especially after constantly feeling ignored but I continued to hold to that belief of a higher power. Even in spite of my backward ways I respected that belief which has proven to produce lifesaving and life changing benefits.

God didn't change my circumstance back then but used it in preparing me for what was to come, the teenage years and beyond. He doesn't create the troubles we face in life, the incorrect use of our free-will does that. Most hardships are produced by our bad choices or the bad choices of others who affect our lives. Approaching seventeen God and church became shelfed in the rear of my mind but never forgotten. Leaning on my own understanding it was finally time to break out and spread my wings.

Surprised by my mother's consent to allow me to leave home I signed up for Job Corps in South Jersey, a trade school for mostly those who for whatever reason didn't complete high school. Here we were able to achieve a GED plus learn a trade, however it seemed for many including myself it was more of a means of escape. So many new faces all with one thing in common, we all had an unpleasant story to tell. There for thirteen months I didn't learn much for multiple reasons, one being my first time away from home the overwhelming feeling of freedom dominated my senses.

At this point I was no longer physically and ver-bally abused but the memories were still very much alive. Now able to distance myself I felt a new awak-ening. However upon my arrival I found myself still yet faced with disappointment at the door learning the trade I was assured was available which was air-condition and refrigeration technician actually wasn't. Having to pick auto mechanic as an alter-nate option after already having my mind set only helped to reinforce what had long become my line of thinking, always expecting the worst so disappointment wouldn't take me by surprise.

Under normal circumstances by the end of my thirteen month stay I should have learned enough to fix any car but there was never any normalcy in my life. Instead of being able to acknowledge the opportunities still in front of me I found it easier to just shut down while continuing to blow in the wind with a whatever attitude. From dropping out of high school to this point and beyond as a way of avoiding disappointment and failure I became accustom to avoiding anything and everything that challenged my abilities.

Being true to myself I don't think anything would have turned out any differently even if I would have been able to take up the trade I first applied for. Still overshadowed by the seeds planted through my adopted mother's words made it easier to use any disappointment as an excuse not to succeed. I was now facing a whole new environment, one I viewed as full of excitement and able to feed my curiosities and I was willing and ready to experience it all. Growing up always feeling out of place and rejected I was continuously searching for acceptance to satisfy my need to belong.

Because of the low opinion I had of myself I was always drawn to elements outside of my own character. From this point on unknowingly I would always be running from myself, always in camouflage, always wearing a mask. Also in seeking acceptance I found myself easily influenced by others. Where I was more restrained because of my upbringing most seemed to be more unrestricted in their thoughts and actions which made it all the more exciting to me. Little did I realize, we were all escaping from something.

During my earlier years running away from home was my only means of escape there were acquaintances who I found to have few if any restrictions on their life. They would help me seek nightly shelter but also was my introduction to petty crimes such as car thief and breaking and entering neighborhood stores, gas stations and such so I wasn't completely naïve. However now a little older things were about to jump to a whole new level. It's been close to fifty years and Tony still crosses my mind from time to time. He was the first brother I became friends with in Job Corps.

Formerly an army base converted into a trade school for young males sixteen to twenty-one years of age Tony and I became such close friends we adopted each other as family. In becoming more familiar with each other I found our backgrounds weren't that different in terms of physical and verbal abuse but I didn't see in him the damage that I saw in myself. Where I displayed little confidence in myself and was more withdrawn he was more vocal and outgoing, in fact I admired his gift of gab and a slickness he had about himself. Tony kept things exciting and that just what I was looking for.

It seemed we were always going where we shouldn't go doing things we shouldn't be doing and I'd just go with the flow. I think in many ways we complimented each other, we had similar personalities, mild mannered and could get along with anyone. However he was more of an open book whereas I was more mysterious, harder to figure out. Another thing that wasn't new to me was getting high however alcohol and marijuana had been my limit of experience. Where the school was located there was only a small grocery store entering the next nearby town about a mile up the road.

You may ask what anyone could find in such a place to get high or even drunk on, for the extreme it was Robitussin cough syrup and Tony fell into that category. He loved getting high and as time passed it would become our favorite pastime but as I said earlier, there was a limit to my madness. I tried the cough syrup but for the most part I'd pass mainly because of the taste however later I would allow myself to be led into worse things which I fell right into.

During the weekdays we were not allowed to leave the grounds therefore those who indulged would jump the fence in the evenings to make their Robitussin run. On weekends if we weren't restricted for one reason or other we could put in for a weekend pass. Tony and I had met some brothers from Jersey City and soon that's where we would end up most of our weekends. Once classes ended on Friday evenings we were off to the races. All between sixteen to eighteen years of age our routine was running the streets, bar hopping and getting high.

Also in the City was what use to be a large hospital now converted into a Job Corps for females housing over a hundred females from all the U.S, needless to say we also spent time popping in and out of there. Having strict rules our visits were limited. However sometimes they would host dances in a large hall within the building which was always a treat. With all this activity I was having the time of my life. Little did I realize I was in the path of a whirlwind slowly picking up velocity, the more vacuum produced the more I was being sucked in.

One of those weekends in Jersey City I found myself confronted with my first introduction to a speedball, heroin and cocaine. I'd sniffed a little cocaine when it was offered to me but this was totally different, this involved hypodermic needles. When it was offered I was in shock for a few seconds. I remember every time my parents would take me to the family doctor he'd always stick me in my backside with a needle and because of that I became to hate needles.

Now I found myself undeterred from allowing someone not even a doctor to stick me with a hypodermic and inject me with street drugs. I knew Tony, I didn't really know the person who was injecting me but if everyone else was still alive and kicking, why not. Allow me to paint a visual picture of the hell I escaped only by the grace of God. I remained on this path for over fifteen years off and on. Along the way I've watched many around me including Tony in a matter of months become addicted which seemed not hard to do.

Unlike most street drugs heroin is a physical addiction where your body needs it to function properly. If that craving is not fed your whole body literally feels the painful effects. It can take up to seven days of agonizing pain before escaping its clutches but few rarely do.

Many times depending on how long a person has been using drug centers and rehabs may have to supply a daily substitute even after going through withdrawal symptoms. If you've never witnessed a heroin addict go through withdrawal you never do, it's a terrible ordeal to witness. The visible physical damage caused by long term usage can be just as terrifying. Something I wouldn't wish on my worst enemy. It wasn't until leaving Job Corps that I became more of an intravenous drug user. When Tony found out I was leaving he shared he had family not far from where I lived and so we ended up leaving together. However somehow I ended up bringing him home with me without even informing my parents. Upon our arrival I was shocked to see how my mother without question welcomed him in. as for my father usually whatever my mother decided in the home he went along with. I could hardly believe how mellowed out she had become. What was only supposed to be a couple weeks turned into a year, I guess it wasn't much of an issue because we were rarely there. Besides my mother fall in love with him because he was very respectful and for the most part he was just a likeable person.

After a few months he finally got in contact with his nearby family and we all got together at their home, this was when the heroin and cocaine use became more frequent. I quickly graduated from having to have someone stick me with the hypodermic to being able to do it with ease myself. You would never have been able to tell I once had a real dislike for needles and now years later if you see how I react when a nurse has to give me a shot you'd never believe I use to inject myself almost on a daily bases.

Before leaving for job corps I had gotten myself into a bit of trouble and expecting a letter for court but left for job corps before receiving the letter. After finding out I was back home I received the letter, already knowing the charge was for breaking and entering to me the crime wasn't that serious. Even though I was close to eighteen it was a juvenile offence with no weapons or violence involved because as I said there were limits to my madness. I opened the envelope and removed the notice, I seen appear in court and then I saw the words "grand jury" and all of a sudden I went into a panic.

I had been to juvenile court a few times but never a grand jury, the only grand jury I knew of was what I saw on TV like Perry Mason. Grand jury where they made you sit next to the judge and ask all these questions while a bunch of other people sitting to the side in a box listened and then surrendered a verdict.

This was big time, I could go to prison. All I could think of was I needed to do something and quick. A couple days later I found myself at the army recruiting office and a week later after passing the physical and written test I was off to the army. Finding out I was being sent to Fort Knox in Kentucky was fine with me, I was on the run so the further the better. A busload of us arrived in early afternoon, we were instructed to exit the bus and line up. Afterwards we were led to a building where we received further instructions.

From there we were led to our temporary barracks. For the following week we lived easy going around collecting our gear, going to a few classes, eating good and lodging. None of us had any idea what was coming, in fact I was thinking oh man this is sweet. We all knew there was more to it than we had already experienced, we just didn't know what or when. We had reached the end of our first week and now we're all wondering what's next. In the earlier meeting we were informed that by the end of that week we'd be moved to our temporary home for an eight weeks basic training course, I thought we had already begun.

It was about eight or nine at night, we were all relaxing and joking around when all of a sudden the doors flew open and the drill sergeants came storming in the building. They were yelling while barking orders for us to get outside and line up. All of us caught by surprise we were scrambling trying to comply with the orders being yelled at us. These sergeants weren't nice like the ones who met us at the bus and took us around the past week. These cats seemed like they were hyped up on something.

As we stood outside lined up in three of four columns they were walking through the aisles in an intimidating manner telling us stuff like we're not home anymore and mama caught help us. I'm wondering why we would need help.

There was few chubby guys in line and they seem to receive the brunt of the abuse being hit in the belly while some strange guy is in your face yelling, and then being forced to get down and do pushups. An hour ago we were laughing and joking and now half of us were crying.

I wasn't exactly sure what I was signing up for but it defiantly wasn't this, and this was just the beginning. My stuttering was still a big problem for me and stressful situations just made it worse. Running from one thing I had ran into the most stressful circumstance I could be in, and the more I thought about it the more stressed I'd become. I wasn't alone because a couple guys tried leaving that night but got caught. There was no way of avoiding, nowhere to hide and seemingly no way out.

I realized at the very first time I had to verbally respond to our drill sergeant and I couldn't get my words out I was going to catch hell just trying to get through the next eight weeks of basic training. In my escape I had jumped from the frying pan into the fire and man was it hot. Something had to give and soon cause I wasn't going to make it, this was definitely not the place for me.

One day I was chewing gum in formation which is against regulations so I had to give twenty-five pushup and before returning to standing position we're supposed to ask, "Permission to recover drill sergeant" but I couldn't get the words out so I just got up. Because I didn't ask permission I had to do another twenty-five. After the twenty-fifth count I just stayed in the pushup position trying to get the words out, at the same time the drill sergeant becoming upset was yelling at me to ask permission. The guys were aware of my problem but not knowing the situation the drill sergeant thought I was being defiant.

He finally told me to get up and then jumped in my face. Already heated myself the guys in line could see my hands closing up to fists. The drill sergeant also noticing began trying to push more buttons saying, "oh, you want to hit me, you think you can take me, go ahead, I want you to". At the same time I'm hearing the guys, don't do it, don't do it". I knew their advice was more sensible so I didn't.

My most humiliating moment was being summoned to the company commander's office. Each one of us was summoned so the commander could meet us and knowing my discomfort verbalizing with people in authority I was dreading my turn. Finally it came, as I'm walking out of my barrack to the commander's building I'm repeating what I'm supposed to say over and over. The routine was I knock, walk in, stand at attention, salute and say, " private Sims reporting as ordered sir", sound's simple and it was for most people, unfortunately I wasn't in that category.

I stood there at attention saluting for what seemed like forever trying to get out the first word. Finally we both gave up, I gave up trying and he gave up trying to help. I left his office feeling like a real fool. Another incident not involving verbal communication happened at night. We were at the rifle range with a different drill sergeant lying face down shooting at targets. At the end of the stage and the sergeant gives the order to stop firing we stop at that point.

Everyone was supposed to have emptied their magazine which I did but I still had a round in the chamber I hadn't fired. The drill sergeant now walking in front between us and the targets instructed we lay down our weapons. I was a little unsure of what to do, should I lay it down or just wait until he gets to me and let him know the situation. Trying to figure it out and not paying attention when he reached me I had no idea how close he was.

Before I knew it I was holding my weapon which still had an unfired round in the chamber which was now pointed in his direction. He began yelling as he took the rifle from my hands. When he checked to find a round in the chamber he flipped. Still lying face down he grabbed me by the shoulders of my jacket, picked me straight up and through me on my back and in a blink of an eye he was on top of me accusing me of trying to shoot him.

Things blew over that night because I think he knew I wasn't trying to shoot him, it was in the heat of the moment of what could have happened. The army and me were not a good fit at all, I remember we had to stay outside for three days as part of our training. It was rainy and muddy the whole time.

We were sleeping in tents and eating food out of cans that looked older than any of us. While out there they gave us an exercise to do, carrying an ammunition box through a wooded area from point A to point B. As I said it had been rainy and muddy the whole time and now two to a box had to follow a trail through a wooded mudded area just to see if we could. Nobody said there would be a steep mudded hill we had to climb. Fighting this hill with me in the rear of the box my partner and I are slipping and sliding trying to get some traction.

There was a handle on each end of the box so with one hand we were trying to secure the box while trying to climb with the other. About half way up my partner let the box go and it slid back catching my ankle. Fed up with the whole exercise once we got the box to the top of the hill I told him I was carrying it another step and he drug it the rest of the way by himself and I didn't care. In fact they had to wait for me because everyone was back accept me. I was so upset I took my time walking back because like I said, I didn't care, I'd had enough of playing GI Joe.

I knew before joining the army that people with flat feet couldn't serve because their feet couldn't withstand the vigorous strain. We would march for miles up and down steep roads in full gear, a back-pack providing everything needed for survival, a hard plastic helmet covered by a steal helmet, heavy combat boots along with our issued riffle hanging from our shoulders. The marching never bothered me but I would witness some who were pushed to their limit dropping from exhaustion. I began thinking maybe if I started complaining about my feet bothering me to the point of not being able to perform properly they'd let me out.

After my complaint and reviewing my performance records I think they also concluded this wasn't a good fit. Because we seemed to be in agreement about me not belonging there after seeing a doctor who approved my discharge the rest of the process went smoothly. Two weeks before graduation from basic training I was leaving. Guys were trying to talk me into staying but I didn't belong there. I was a non-violent person by nature and didn't even like guns. I must have been out of my mind when I thought this up.

After all that hell I put myself through I still ended up having to face a grand jury. However I didn't have to sit in the witness booth and there was no jury in the jury box. For a short time I confined myself to a prison of my own making. Running from what I had convinced myself could happen led me to a symbolized prison already in existence but not made for me. I didn't have to be there, I volunteered.

I walked out just receiving probation but it was an experience I won't forget anytime soon. After Job Corps and the army I hadn't achieved anything that would move my life forward, I was still right where I began. About six months after being home I decided to take a chance applying for Job Corps a second time. The age range for attending was sixteen to twenty-one, close to reaching twenty-two I wasn't even sure if I had a chance. I submitted my application and waited for a reply. The reply came in the form of a request that I write a letter explaining why I wanted a second chance.

I wrote the letter telling how I realized I wasted a great opportunity and knowing if I had another chance I'd get it right this time. I guess they like what I wrote because my application was accepted. What I wrote must have sounded good but unfortunately it wasn't as sincere as I wish it should have been. The fact is I just want to get away. I was always running, never sure what from but always running. Either I was afraid to or just couldn't seem to grasp the concept of responsibility. While applying we were given the choice of in-state or out of state and choosing out of state in a few weeks I was off to Indiana where I remained for seven months.

The only trade they had I thought might capture my interest and maybe change my perspective was building maintenance. It was interesting but not enough. I even went for my GED again but sorry to say things only repeated itself, I didn't learn anything because I was too busy doing what pleased me which in the long run didn't add up to much. I look back now and think, I've had plenty chances in my life and wasted them all because as old as I was I still didn't know any better. What other excuse could I give that would make any sense? Tony had moved out of my parent's house before I returned from the army into a rooming house taking most of my clothes with him.

He'd convinced my mother by the time I got home I'd be too big to fit anything and she listened to him. However he made up for it when I returned from Job Corps by getting me a job with him working for a cleaning service. It was like a family affair, everyone working there except the owner were heroin addicts. Most of them couldn't work a regular forty hour week if their life depended on it.

We worked mostly after hours stripping and waxing floors in closed supermarkets and malls. The smaller accounts like offices or beauty salons would be split up between us. We were all making good money, anywhere from four to six hundred tax free each week.

There were great perks, good money tax free, able to borrow against our pay through the week and that was good because most of them needed a package before work, and sometimes even at work. Although I didn't need to as they did I still enjoyed the high. So when they'd get their package I'd join in also. It was something about getting high together having a similar experience at the same time, like drug brothers.

We loved the jobs supermarkets because we could go to the deli section and make our own sandwiches not to mention the shelves full of goodies. We were some crew but always got the job done and done well. Just reflecting back to how empty and weak the person within was, in spite of my dislike for needles just to see how easily I gave into shooting drugs was the sign of a person who didn't care much about himself. I could have easily ended up another unfortunate soul who reached a point of no return.

I was in a dangerous place and even being able to keep my head above water I've experienced some close calls which could have ended very badly. Sharing a couple of those experiences, one sunny afternoon a few of us were in a second floor apartment getting high and I overdosed. Passed out in the apartment the two others dragged me down the flight of stairs, down the porch stairs and to the car. When I came to I was leaned up against the car groggy and sore as hell from being dragged, however it could have turned out so much worse.

Another instance took place during a visit from my cousin Nick, his mother which was unusual and Nick's lady friend came to visit. I happen to be at my parent's house when they showed up. I was well aware of Nick's drugs problems and seeing another cousin in the car, Michelle who they'd picked up locally was in deep herself, at that point I knew something was up. At the time there was a highly potent strand of heroin out Nick had heard about but wasn't in Baltimore. While he was here he wanted to see for himself what the talk was all about.

One thing about addicts is they take their heroin straight up and most are able to go on their way right afterwards. Being a drug that has a down effect it sends a casual user like myself into deep nods, it's like dozing off for about fifteen to thirty seconds at a time, going in and out for about an hour. Therefore my choice was always a mixture of heroin and cocaine and even then I may still go through the nod thing but not as bad. Michelle knew where to get it and I knew somewhere in the area to go and do it.

Since they were heroin addicts there would be no cocaine included so if I wished to indulge it would be straight up. Hey who was I to argue, I'd never been one to turn down a chance to get high. So now we have the package and we're at the destination pre-paring to enjoy our high. All of them sitting on the edge of the bed Nick was the first one ready to put it to the test. While Nick's lady friend and Michelle was enjoying theirs I had mine prepared and waiting for one of them to finish. All of a sudden as I also sat down on the bed we felt a thump behind us, we turned around and Nick was out. He had overdosed.

With my portion in the hypodermic ready to go I quickly put it down to the side, grabbed Nick and pulled him outside. I began slapping his face until he finally came to. After things had calm down I went back to enjoy mine. Afterwards although I never said anything I realized no one but Michelle had also done mine while I was with Nick and replaced it with water, which turned out to be a blessing in disguise. No one especially Nick was in any condi-tion to drive back so the only other in the car with a license and not impaired I drove the six miles back to the house.

I think about if Michelle hadn't done what she did we may not have made it back to the house because I know I would have been nodding off and on behind the wheel which could have ended very badly and not just for us. Unfortunately both passed years ago due to aids but I remember, I used the same needle they used meaning I could have just as easily been in that number. I have no doubt God was with me through many seen as well as unseen dangers that could have easily turned fatal. That's why I hold tight to **Romans 8-28, <u>God causes all things </u>to work together for good to those who love God, those who are called according to His purpose**.

It holds a lot of truth in my life because although I couldn't see it then I've experienced it time and again. From the late seventies traveling with Tony and others across the bridge to Harlem to purchase our drugs we'd also stop in what was referred to as shooting galleries. They were found in rows of abandon apartment building where addicts stayed and made their hustle selling and renting needles and space to get high.

Going through the whole experience I'd witness up close and personal the true physical and mental horrors created from heavy heroin use, the more I saw the more determined I became to never allow myself to become a slave to this drug. Strangely though, the horrors didn't change my direction.

Journey Into Self-Discovery

$\mathcal{I}$ *think about* how easy it is to believe it won't or can't happen to us and how so many found out the hard way. I just thank God my determination remained a reality because although I wasn't physically addicted in every other way I was just as out of control. After a long run together Tony and I gradually began just drifting in and out. Unlike so many I was able to back away whenever from my heroin and cocaine use without having to bare serious consequences. However drugs overall would become my best friend keeping me camouflaged and carefree, providing escape from the insecure person I've always worked to conceal.

I realize today that most of my insecurities during this time came from my choice to dwell in an element I never belonged. I guess I sensed it from the beginning but this path required less effort making it more comfortable, a place where I didn't have to be me. For the next twenty plus years I would bounce from one drug to the next, whatever drug was in season I'd be there to join in on the celebration. All through the eighties to mid-nineties there was a variety of drugs floating around to pick and choose from. I'd always been willing to try anything once, if it didn't agree with me I never touched it again but it wasn't too often I met a drug I didn't like.

Years ago I'd reached a point of no longer being able to see my life without drugs, the picture looked empty because there was nothing else to fill the emptiness within. I would go around patting myself on the back for all the years not being addicted to anything and maintaining control, but in reality I was far from in control because I was allowing the drugs to define my identity. By the late eighties into the nineties cocaine had become my main choice but in no way did I restrict myself. However while many outside of the hardcore scene were into sniffing for me it was a waste, it just didn't compare with that sudden impact I was use to experiencing from injecting it.

These were also the months that I would find my life turned upside down bringing me to my knees. Tony and I were still hanging out at times, one evening doing our usual his cousin was across the room smoking something from a small glass tube, this was a first for me. I ask him about it and if I could try it.

He told me it was crack cocaine then I watched him put a small white pebble in the tube and take some first, I guess the tube was empty when he passed it because I didn't get anything out of it. I wasn't sure what I was supposed to feel but after that I viewed it as a waste I didn't give it another thought.

A few weeks later I found myself observing someone cooking cocaine using baking soda and water in a miniature bottle forming what resembled a white stone and seemed just as hard. After watching the intake process with the glass tube I followed their lead, cocaine being my preferred drug anyway this high was even more intense than shooting it. That day after a few more hits I heard myself speak out for all sitting around to hear saying, "this drug is straight from the pits of hell". I believed it had to be because the high was too good.

As I look back I think wow, a clear warning coming from my own mouth, I believe it was God speaking to my spirit and without thought I just blurted out what my spirit was receiving. Yet I chose to ignore that clear warning but that was nothing new for me especially when drugs were involved. I wasn't worried, I had been able to keep myself in check thus far and now shouldn't be any different. Remember what I said earlier about fooling ourselves, I was about to experience a rude awakening. Because of the harsh treatment experienced during my childrearing years I remained insecure in my ability to interact verbally with those I viewed as authority figures.

Even at the thought such as having to think about an upcoming job interview would have me stressed. I would already see myself sitting across from the interviewer with my nerves on edge trying not to stutter as I spoke. Another strike against me was how I avoided eye contact. I had read somewhere that interviewers were more likely to choose a person who looked at them while speaking because it displays confidence, which I surely lacked. Interviews felt like being sat under a bright spotlight and being interrogated. However I found I could avoid job interviews working though temporary employment agencies allowing my character and work ethics to speak for me.

When applying with an agency I always made it known I preferred an assignment that could lead to a permanent position and that's how I landed some real good jobs through most of my work history. Jobs I never would have gotten if I had to go through a regular interview.

I worked as a temporary employee for the very first cellphone company in NJ, after working a year in the mailroom I was offered a permanent position. Moving me from the mailroom to a higher position in a year the company had grown so fast the owners gave everyone a five thousands dollar bonus just before selling the company along with our secured employment to AT&T. If I would have had to go through a traditional interview I would have never made it pass the front door and this is just one example which confirms I wasn't dumb but neither was I in my right mind.

I had become a master of disguise with the ability to make those outside my warped world see what I wanted them to see, a person in control of his life. Before AT&T I had gotten a job with a small office cleaning business through the employment agency. By this time I still loved my cocaine but I'd put aside the needle and was cooking my own crack cocaine. In a short time things had gotten serious, I had gone from the small glass stem to a glass pipe and from a lighter to a miniature torch.

During this time I had moved to Hackensack living with a woman named Joyce I had met on a previous temporary job assignment. Living in a rooming house at the time wasn't bad but it wasn't great either. Although I wasn't a heroin addict I was living the life of one because that's all I hung around. Meeting this nice looking middle aged woman not affiliated with any of this with a seemingly good job, her own ride which I didn't have, and apartment with no live-in kids sounded ideal.

However the grass is not always greener on the other side which I found out in the worst way. Like I shared earlier there were no live-in kids which made it sound all the more ideal. The next thing I knew it's a month later and with no warning a grown man appears with suitcases.

Her son Larry was in his early thirties, 6'2 at about 210lbs, I guess you could conclude my ideal picture was severely cracked and you'd be correct. A smoker himself in no time he took it to a whole new level and I allowed myself to be sucked right in. As his habit begin to progress people would be in and out all hours because he welcomed it. All who came there to smoke had to feed the house, the house being him. Arguments would take place regularly because he was the type who tried to do more of your drugs than you. It wouldn't be long before I'd find myself in the midst of them from time to time.

After they met me many would try to bypass him wanting rather to deal with me as the house, and that's how I allowed myself to be sucked into the madness, my love for drugs along with the opportunities for the free high. If they needed him to make a run while drugs were still floating around he wouldn't leave in fear he may miss out. Then he or someone else would ask me which most of them preferred anyway mainly because I was known for bringing them back what they paid for. Not saying I didn't take off the top but I was never greedy, it's not in my character which more times than not played in my favor.

As the house became more noticeable to the police as a potential hot spot it would bring their presence to our doorstep frequently. Their unwanted attention even resulted in a couple raids because they had labeled our home as a crack house. That's how bad things had become. Joyce having no dealings with any of it even got caught up in the midst of one of those raids and locked up for a couple hours for no other reason than having no control over her son or home. My ideal picture was now shattered in pieces. It wasn't long before I began exhibiting addict characteristics like urges, anticipation and irritation. On payday I couldn't wait for the day to be over and when it was things still wasn't moving fast enough for me because I'd be visualizing that first hit.

Another addict characteristic is when the money is funny towards feeding our habit we look for opportunities to be the odds. While cleaning offices

I'd find myself looking in office desk-draws. I played it off as just being nosy until I found what I was really looking for. I took the seven hundred dollars knowing they'd know who it was.

Knowing I was fired and would probably go to jail I left the front door keys on the desk, left the front door unlocked and disappeared for three days. When I showed up dusty and broke and expecting the police to ride up on me sooner or later surprisingly they never did.

The owner of the cleaning service paid back the money to avoid bad publicity. Needless to say I never went back to the job. Although I saw the company vans on the road we never saw each other again which was fine with me. By this time there was no room for lying to myself, I knew I was out of control. A constant twenty plus years uppers, downers, pill, powder, or liquid, I'd always maintained control but now finding myself going way off script making desperate decisions regardless of the cost was madness. Still I tried playing my role in the outside world best I could. A month or so later I was working at a cell-phone company through a temporary agency.

After a year working in the mailroom I guess I'd passed the test because about a month before my assignment was over I was offered a permanent position with the company. Of cause I said yes and after he vouched for me I was in the office as a full time employee. During my time in the mailroom for the most part I was able to restrict my smoking for weekends. On paydays I had my routine of getting home as soon as possible, grabbing Joyce's car and off to purchase my party favorite. An addict presented with a chance to get high regardless of what day it is will more than likely fall right in line, and that was my downfall.

It didn't take long before the wall began cracking and my usage begin slowly overflowing into my weeknights. I'd find myself up at 5or6 in the morning from the night before having to be at work by 8:30, I don't need to but I'll say it anyway, by 10:30 I was like a zombie. Imagine being in an office setting sitting behind a desk going through paperwork while struggling desperately to keep your eyes open, believe me it's the worst. I worked for AT&T two years before being let go for getting caught twice sleeping in the bathroom stall, caught because I was snoring.

Afterwards full of anger and self-pity life took a turn for the worse. I was angry at myself for allowing myself to become so out of control even after the first words out my mouth describing this drug was it's straight from the pits of hell. I'd done more than my share of a variety of drugs but none had ever come with such a clear warning.

I was right where deep down I always felt I should be minus the crack cocaine and now because of my stupidity everything's shot to hell and to twist the knife a little more I kept reminding myself I had no one to blame but myself. As anger turned to disgust I began running more toward than from what I perceived as the source of my problems. I began finding it difficult working regular forty hour a week jobs because of my sleeping habits. Sometimes I'd be lucking if I got thirty- six hours of sleep during the course of a week. It became nothing new for me to disappear two or three days at a time with Joyce's car stuck in the madness of the constant chase.

I would manage to find hustle work where I got paid at the completion of the job and that would be my crack plus money. You may ask what's plus, plain and simple crack cocaine turned me into a sexual freak. I share this because this was not me, I'd gone well beyond out of control. Unlike the physical addiction of constant heroin use this was psychological therefore I had become a slave in my own mind. A warning I never expected comes from my own mouth from only heaven knows where, straight from the pits of hell, still the warning was falling on deaf ears.

I was in my late thirties during this time, Joyce was about six or seven years older than I and her son Larry was about seven or eight years younger than I. I look back sometimes at the things I used to put her through and it hurts me to my heart because I know in no way did she deserved any of it. Disappearing with her vehicle for days at a time, stealing from her, catching me with other women and still she held on and why I'll never know. As scary as I know it would have been for me at the time I wish she would have thrown me out, at least the hurt for her would have been short lived instead of prolonged.

I always felt bad afterwards because none of it was ever my intension, I was literally out of my mind.

I suddenly began finding myself in and out of county jails serving between one to nine months mostly on drug related offenses or either non-payment of child support. I have a funny story concerning child support at my front door, however it wasn't funny at the time.

An acquaintance and I were at my home one evening, riding with him earlier that day he had hustled up some cash. Now back at the house the plan was he'd take the ride to purchase the party favorites while I lay back because dinner was about to be served. While he's gone there's a knock at the door which wasn't at all unusual. Not bothering to check I opened the door to find myself face to face with two detectives. Now I'm thinking "ahhhhh damn, what now".

They showed me the photo of a person I'd never seen before who supposedly lived at this address, after confirming that no such person lived at this address they turned and left. A few minutes later another knock and again without checking I opened the door. It's the same two detectives but this time they had a different photo, this one was of me. The detective with the photo in hand and a nonchalant expression said, "Oh we're sorry, we had the wrong photo before, you're the person we're looking for".

With all the heat that was on the house because of the traffic in and out all hours of the day and night I should have been more on the alert but I missed the slick move. Before the detectives attempted their arrest they first wanted to confirm I was home and secondly they wanted to see what type of person they were dealing with, would I be trouble or was I more on the mild-mannered side. I was looking forward to that dinner and the party favorites that were on the way. I remember the pork chops just about to come out of the frying pan. What was looking to be a beautiful evening was shot to hell in less than five minutes.

Because of the drugs offenses I had my driver's license revoked just adding another category of constantly getting caught driving without a license to my already growing list of charges.

I remember the evening clearly as if it was yesterday being so overwhelmed with hopelessness that I gathered up all my drug paraphernalia, walked to the police station, set it all on the front desk in front of the officer and told him I didn't want to do this anymore, I need help. Each time I'd been incarcerated I told myself I would use the time to get my head screwed on straight but once I got out I soon found myself on the chase like I was making up for lost time.

The officer at the front desk made a call and soon afterwards a detective came from the back. We talked briefly and then he gave me his card with a number he'd written on the back to a drug rehab facility. I went there not caring what the outcome would be, all I knew at this point was I didn't want to live the life I was living another day. First thing the following day I called the number hoping for quick results but instant I was setup with an appointment for a week later. Needless to say I was right back at it the following day.

I was still getting it in on the day of my appointment up till the very end. While in the waiting area I found myself making a couple bathroom runs finishing up the last of what I had then throwing the stem in the garbage. After speaking with the counselor I found out the program was only a twenty-eight day detox which did little for a crack addict except to supply a pause period. As much as I truly desired my freedom once my month was up in less than two week I was off to the races again. Life was becoming unbearable as despair and regret began to overwhelm me. What have I done, how did I get here and how do I find my way out, questions but no answers.

Eventually I did end up in another drug rehab and I bet you'd never guess where, within the county jail. Yep, more drugs charges. I remember going to court and pleading guilty and when returning for sentencing the judge, a brother said, Mr. Sims, I see you've been in front of a judge quite a few times but never really done any time. Up until then including my petty drug offences I hadn't done any more than three months for non-payment of child support and that was time enough, too much if you ask me but I guess he didn't see it that way.

He said I'm giving you two hundred and seventy days, I'm thinking two hundred and seventy days, what kind of sentence is that? I had plenty time figuring out how long it was in months while they were leading me away. A month into the nine months I went back to court on another petty drug charge which added another three months. I had never seen myself as a criminal although I had done things that could be considered criminal. Mainly I was just a person who enjoyed illegal drugs.

As long as my record had become there was never any weapons or any type of violence involved, just my love for drugs that sometimes caused me to overstep boundaries. Anyway, about five months in lockup I heard those in for drug use and with no violent offences were eligible to apply for a three months drug rehab within but apart from the rest of the inmate population. My mindset from the beginning was to use the time forced on me wisely but thus far there was no plan of how to go about it, I guess I was hoping time would do it for me.

This opportunity was uplifting and a blessing in more ways than one. In my early forties I was locked in a dormitory with thirty-nine other guys with the majority in their late twenties and under. With most seemingly familiar with each other unfamiliar faces especially those out of the age range. Some including myself would find our packages stolen while we were at the chow hall or in the yard. I'd come back knowing only with bed space no matter how good I tried to hide anything it would be gone. Each time I'd make it known I didn't like it while even adding threatening remarks.

Less than a week before my transfer one of the guys I'd become cool with had his blanket stolen by one of the younger guys. After sleeping that night with just a sheet the following day knowing which one it was the guy stayed in the dorm during lunch, while the one who stole the blanket in the first place was at lunch the one who had it stolen took his blanket back. That night three guys jumped him. The one who started it all and who was with two other guys couldn't let that go because it's all about image especially in a place like this, he had a duty to maintain and display his toughness.

It wasn't the first such attack I'd witnessed, days before this incident the same young boys attacked a white guy who played cards with us because he started refusing they're request for cigarettes. After this last attack which was moving in a very uncomfortable direction I began sensing it was just a matter of time. A couple days after the blanket incident they called my name to pack up for movement, I was ready to hold my own but I'm glad I didn't have to. Reaching my destination the environment I walked into was as different as day and night from where I had been moved from.

The floors shined like glass and everything looked clean. It was like a breath of fresh air. This smaller dorm held twenty guys sectioned off by cubicles designed to house two to a cube. We were given uniforms instead of the traditional jumpsuits, and even had our own yard. Although we were still in jail it didn't feel like it. We had no further contact with the rest of the inmates unless we broke the rules. Fighting, stealing and frequent insubordination were the main ones that earned us a ticket back no if, and, or buts, and none of us wanted that. Two guys were sent back while I was there for punches being thrown.

One of them must have did or said something he shouldn't have before he left the dorm he had come from because he began crying and pleading not to send him back. I felt for him but we all knew the rules. We were given special privileges like being able to order certain snacks the other inmates weren't able to like bread, peanut butter and jelly, it may not sound like much and on the outside it would probably be the last thing on our mind to eat but jail gives you a different perspective on things.

Being there during the Thanksgiving and Christmas holidays another privilege I got to experience was the meals catered in by the churches and organizations who helped to sponsor the program. I spent my last three months attending drug counseling classes and doing whatever I had to too make it through the program to my release date. I was excited about my release but not so much about heading back to the place I called home. I hadn't really expected anything to have changed, if anything it had gotten worse and I wasn't far off.

It was still a hot spot and no place for a person in recovery to be. I wouldn't be long before I was all in once again. I remember as a much younger man in a conversation and suicide was mentioned. I remember saying I would never try and take my life and only a weak minded person would. I still feel that way but no longer in a judgmental mindset. Unless we've walked in that person's shoes we can never understand what led them to that point, what led him to giving up the fight. I was driving to the house one night after being out the two previous nights.

I had left the house with Joyce's car supposedly to pick up my party favorite and back although I had been known to sometimes be gone for hours, other times for days and this was one of those times. Upon heading back I began looking at myself, I had left the house with money in my pocket looking and feeling good and now I only seen someone broke, busted, and disgusted. Driving with my focus on myself the one thought that wrapped it all together overwhelming was, "I had no one to blame but myself" not just for this incident but for it all. I could have removed myself from the environment at any time if not for already being drained by the lifestyle I was so familiar with living.

Even though the drastic change in living arrangement that took place in the beginning should have set off warning bells I guess not wanting to throw in the towel without testing the waters first caused me to ignore that warning, and the longer I stayed the weaker I became until becoming part of the madness. I had been in drug rehabs and even incarcerated for months at a time but always ended up right back where I left off. Anger, regret, hopelessness, helplessness and on, the overwhelming emotions filled my existence with such darkness I began seeing only one last hope which was to end it all.

When I looked over my life I seen nothing but emptiness, I existed but for what? From the time I stepped out on my own drugs became the highlight of my life. There was no purpose, no direction, no rhyme or reason, only confusion. Maybe my adopted mother was right, maybe I wasn't meant to be here, maybe I was just a mistake and that's why from the beginning my life had been nothing but a living hell. At that point all I witnessed was a dead man walking.

Without wasting any more time the decision was made and now the question was how. My first thought was cutting my wrist which sounded as good as any.

I needed something very shape, a razor blade was more than sufficient but without a penny in my pocket I knew what I had to do. I pulled into a supermarket parking lot going inside with the sole purpose of stealing a pack of razorblades and maybe a snack since I was also hungry, wasn't no sense going out on an empty stomach. I was that at ease with what I was about to do, in my mind I was gaining, not losing because I felt I had nothing to lose.

In the store I grabbed a pack of blades and a pack of lunchmeat. Unfortunately I was caught on camera and stopped at the door. Led to a back room I was asked to remove the items, once they saw what I had taken they began making jokes asking me if I was planning to shave while eating a sandwich. At this point I cared little about being arrested but they released me with a warning never to show my face in the store again or I would be. However I was far from giving up, there was more than one store that had what I needed.

At another store I managed to get half of what I wanted, what was most important, the razor blades. I drove back to the supermarket parking lot which seemed to be the perfect place, it was dark, late with very little traffic on foot or wheels. Picking my spot I parked the vehicle. As I reflected over my life I began asking God to forgive me for allowing my life to become so out of control, to forgive me for the person I'd become. As tears began to fall I cried out even more asking Him to please forgive me for what I was about to do while telling my love ones who had already passed on that I was on my way hoping to see them soon.

As I worked towards getting up enough nerve to stand the pain the plan was to cut my wrist and then lay back allowing sleep to overtake me not expecting to wake, not in this life anyway. Apparently I didn't muster up enough nerve to cut deep enough because I woke the following morning. Opening my eyes to a pool of blood where my arm rested I sat up. Looking around to only face another failure I began crying like a baby, not because of what I attempted but because I failed. I couldn't even succeed in killing myself, could my life get any more hopeless.

There seemed to be no escape, the only conclusion to this life is that I was destine to suffer. After that episode it was back to life as usual as if it never happened. Only something straight from the pits of hell would cause anyone to quickly ignore such a destructive episode as attempting suicide to go back to what led you to that point in the first place. After about a month again I was on my way home after disappearing for a couple days. A few blocks from my destination I happen to see one of Larry's friends.

He informed me Larry was highly upset making verbal threats because I had interrupted his flow of free drugs by disappearing with the vehicle. After that news I decided to park a block away and have the friend go to the house and tell Joyce to come meet me. As I'm standing outside the vehicle waiting I saw Larry running down the street towards me. I was 5'11 at 160lbs while he weighed in at 6'2 at about 210lbs and at least eight years younger therefore when I spotted him I jumped in the vehicle and locked all the doors. As he got closer to where I could see the deadly look on his face I started the vehicle.

As I witnessed the yelling and cursing while pulling on the doors I put the vehicle in drive. Seeing what I was about to do he jumped on the hood of the vehicle yelling threats and that's when I hit the gas pedal. The next thing I know I'm flying down the street and he's flying off the hood landing in the middle of a dark intersection. As I looked in the rear view mirror seeing him getting up I felt relieved knowing he wasn't seriously hurt. When his mother was finally able to come retrieve her vehicle she told me when he returned home he told her I tried to kill him.

They said he wanted Joyce to call the police because he wanted to press charges against me but she told him to do it. With all the run-ins he'd had with the cops he really didn't want that. However that's when I made up my mind I wasn't going back.

Not so much because of what I might have had to face but more so because things could have went terribly wrong and I could have been facing a lengthy prison sentence for something I never meant to do and that scared me even more. I'm old school, we know losing a fight is short lived but a prison sentence is felt for years. I think about a fight we had once before in the middle of the street.

He had gotten on top of me attempting to hold me down but the adrenaline must have been pumping hard because three times I was able to flip him off. After that I guess he said damn this and ran and grabbed a brick. He was younger but I was smaller and quicker, he wasn't gonna catch me, especially with a brick in his hand. However I don't feel it would have turned out quite the same if he could have laid hands on me after getting up off that street intersection.

Although it wasn't my true intention I made it seem as if it was a temporary situation on my part. I remembered once before even though I wasn't, I threatened to leave and she cried asking me not to leave her and it broke my heart, I truly didn't want to go through that again. I asked her to bring me a few couple changes of clothes. When she returned she put me up in a cheap nearby motel for the night which I wasn't expecting. The following day I was able to get information of a nearby homeless shelter where I spent the following week. Although I was officially homeless with the pressure probably reaching a cooling point by then I possibly could have went back but for me that was no longer an option.

Besides this place wasn't bad considering what I had heard or seen on the news concerning homeless shelters. It was three large trailers linked together. When inside you'd never know we were in trailers. The site was equipped with a kitchen and dining area, a TV room, washer and dryer, and designed to house about twenty people, two to a room. I was feeling content for a while. While there I ran into Jesse, a brother I knew from childhood days and also my wife's cousin who was also homeless.

I was surprised because he said he'd been there for a couple weeks and during my five days I'm just seeing him, the place wasn't that big, but he told me he'd been working during the day. We talked awhile telling each other a short version of our story. During the conversation hearing how we were fighting a similar battles I shared how I had recently promised myself I would not put another pipe or stem to my mouth, I was through and likewise he told me he made the same promise to himself. Not long afterwards he shared he had some money and was hoping to go out with a bang.

Remember a few pages back I shared how opportunities always seem to present themselves to weaken and throw us off course to drag us deeper into hell, well that's what happened. After hearing Jesse's proposal and quickly ignoring the promise made to myself I followed in agreement. Not knowing much about the area he asked if I knew somewhere near by to get the party favorite. All I had to do was say no and that would have put a halt to the chain of events in waiting.

Instead knowing a spot not far from where we were I moved in that direction and off we went. After taking care of that business the next question asked was if I knew where we could go, and being the helpful person that I am I led the way. At this point I would like to pause for a minute to explore a spiritual manifestation in the making. You read how me as a boy growing up through my adopted father's example and love for the church I gained the belief of someone or something greater than ourselves which set boundaries in my life.

Even in my lack of knowledge about Him because of my acknowledgement in him God has always been there watching over me which is why I didn't self-destruct. However just like loving earthly parents will bail us out of our mess time after time sooner or later especially if we've been warned but they continue to see no change, although the love is still there they will cease coming to our rescue.

That's how I view my relationship with God, he kept me through all my madness even while so many around me were being overwhelmed and swallowed up. Even a loving and patient God has his limits and I believe I'd reached His. When God stands back leaving us on our own it's like open season for all the bad that could happen to happen. It was as far back as the eighties when I said I would never take my own life and those who did were weak-minded people. When God stepped back I began to feel the full weight of my madness which became unbearable.

Sitting in that vehicle in a dark parking lot on a cold winter night crying like a baby was the very first time I truly talked to God wholeheartedly holding nothing back.

At that point I had nothing to lose and like an open book I laid it all out there, just God and me. I wasn't sure if he heard me, I wasn't even sure if anyone was there to hear but during those moments through blind faith I chose to believe there was a God and that he was hearing me.

From that point a chain of events would take place in my life guiding me straight to Him. First the suicide attempt, then came experiencing homelessness which is where we left off so let's continue. Jesse and I were off to get our smoke on. As we entered the apartment there were others I knew already there and the traffic in and out was constant. Jesse and I going back to replenish were in and out a couple times ourselves. The person who lived there was a little slow and using that to an advantage many were able to abuse his home where as long as he received a little for himself he was happy. Apparently that night the apartment was being watched.

After the last trip Jesse and I made we were sitting on a couch and someone said they thought they heard someone jiggling the doorknob. The guy who lived there went to the door while at the same time some were telling him not to open it. Not thinking much of it he opened the door and the narcotics squad rushed in. At the time I had a stem in my hand which I slid under the couch. Whether anything was found on us or not even though they had no warrant to enter everyone in the apartment was taken to the police station and checked for outstanding warrants.

Neither I nor Jesse had any so we were released with a summons to appear in court but our problems were far from over. The shelter had strict policies which was swiftly enforced. The rule that affected us was breaking curfew which meant losing your spot. By the time we were released from the police station we had already missed curfew by a half hour. Jesse tried to get one of the detectives to write us a note explaining we were late but that wasn't happening.

When we did get back to the shelter we tried to explain but the person at the front desk wasn't hearing it. It was close to 1:00 AM in the dead of winter when we were asked to pack our stuff and be on our way. I was so hurt but the pain was just beginning.

There was no other nearby shelters willing or able to take us in that time of night so we were pretty much hit, up the creek without a paddle. I discovered later that this homeless situation wasn't new to Jesse. I knew no one had forced me to go along with anything but apart from Jesse I wouldn't have been in this mess. At the same time I have to thank God for Jesse because I realized that without his guidance I don't know how I would have made it through the rest of the night and most of that following day without losing my mind.

I was forty-three years old and through all of thirty plus years in my mess I had never experienced homelessness therefore I had no idea what to do or where to go. Maybe if it had happened during the summer it wouldn't had been as scary but this was in the dead of winter when freezing to death was a real possibility. So what do we have so far, I attempted suicide, becoming homeless, residing in a comfortable shelter feeling content even for a while which was not part of God's agenda, and thrown out of the shelter in the dead of winter. God had heard my heartfelt cry as I attempted suicide but wouldn't allow me to die, but He was still at work. You see it was never about Jesse, it was all about me.

During God's reconstructive work on us he uses people, places or things, whatever is needed to help guide us to where He needs us to be and boy was He doing a job on me. God will even use our weaknesses to put us in the position to receive what He wants to do in our life. Jesse reached in his pocket and pulled out a phone number to a homeless hotline, I never would have known there was such a number. Neither of us had cellphones so we found a pay phone and called the eight hundred number. They gave us the number and address of another nearby shelter. Jesse called only to hear that the place was full.

I was broke from the beginning and he had enough money left for two cups of coffee so for the rest of that night until about 5AM we sat in an all-night donut shop nursing our one cup, thank God the counter person didn't complain. At 6AM we went back to the shelter for breakfast, we could eat there we just could no longer sleep there. For the remainder of the day I followed Jesse here and there, wherever heat was available.

I spent more time in the library that one day than I'd spent in the last previous twenty years. Mid-afternoon Jesse made a collect call and soon after-wards dropped the ultimate bomb on me. He was going to stay with his mother a few days who lived in a senior's complex. It felt like the bottom had just dropped from beneath me. He was the guide to my survival, he was my cushion that softened the blow of being thrown out into this freezing hell and now, what would I do, night was quickly approaching, where would I go? As I said God was at work but still my dependence was on the wrong things.

He handed me the phone number to the home-less hotline and was on his way. At that moment a loneliness like I've never felt before came over me, for the first time in my life I felt truly alone in this world. All I had that presented any glimpse of hope was a piece of paper with a phone number Jesse gave me. I had lived in this town for ten years, that's how long I had been living together with Joyce but now the area felt foreign and lonely as if seeing threw a different set of eyes. I felt out of place, how did I ever get here?

After pulling myself together I figured the sooner I call the number the better chance I have of finding shelter for the night. It was about 5PM and get-ting dark, the darker it became the colder it would become and with many places starting to close for the day time was not on my side. Not knowing what to expect I called the number to hear a soft soothing voice on the other end. After telling her my situation see gave me the number and address of two locations, one was a hotel which was walking distance and the other was in Paterson, three towns away. By this time I'd been outside for a while and was truly feeling the cold.

You would think a person facing my circumstance would head for the nearest warm location. However, I can't explain the reasoning, in fact there was no reasoning. All I felt at that moment was the need to reach the location three towns away. The urge was so strong that even in spite of how cold I already was I was willing and actually willing and ready to walk if I had to. Even though it was during the warmer months I had walked this stretch before so I knew my way.

I had even walked quite a long distance during a winter month wearing just a hoody and winter vest from Washington Heights NY over the bridge to Hackensack NJ. So I was willing to do whatever I had to but the path was set. No matter what I think or say or how I think or say it I find no human logic that would explain what was going on within me that evening, I just knew what I felt and the feeling was so intense it couldn't be ignored nor denied. I decided to take a chance and call Joyce, the problem was our phone was off so I'd have to make a collect call to her aunt and uncle's apartment upstairs and hope they accept.

Hearing Joyce's voice on the other end I told her the situation and asked if she would drive me to Paterson. In the next fifteen minutes she was pulling up driving her aunt's car, she told me her son had her car and you know what that meant, nothing had changed. I knew the location of where we were going but it wasn't until we pulled up in front of the large white building that I realized its exact location. We were right in the midst of a drug infested area which I was well familiar with.

This was the area where I mostly came to get my drugs and disappear from home for days at a time. I had walked pass this big white building with the big white sign in the front, "Good Shepherd Mission" a hundred times never paying much attention and now it was the focus of my attention, of all places why here? I was learning through experience there to be a reason behind everything God does and found His reasoning as to my question to be revealed soon. Long before ending up here I had made out this building to be a homeless shelter because at a certain time of day I would see guys gathering outside waiting to get in, little did I know that once inside I would find so much more.

Once inside speaking to the front desk person I was informed that the house functioned under Christian oriented values and asked if I had a problem with it which I didn't. Upon agreeing to the rules of the house then being led to where the shelter guys stayed I was approached by a couple brothers telling me about a program. It definitely sounded like something I wanted to hear. As I listened I was enlightened by the news that this building also functioned as a nine month drug and alcohol rehab. This was news I never expected, I could have never imaged my needs being met in such a way.

The one thing I remember being told by one of the guys was that "it was no accident I ended up there" and those words never left my remembrance because for the most part they seem to fall right in line with all I had been experiencing thus far. Sometimes looking back I fear to think how my life would be today had I not listened to that voice within twenty years ago. That night I requested to be accepted into the program. So let's have another recap: Jesse was removed from the equation but left me a lifeline.

Using that lifeline I received most needed information, once received I had a choice to make, whether I listened and accepted my reasoning or the guidence I had received from deep within. God was at work and I was finally beginning to see His plan unfold. The joy and relief I felt was indescribable. It felt as if the weight of the world had been lifted from my shoulders. For the first in a long time I was able to see a glimmer of light coming from the other end of a long dark tunnel. From that point I was determined that no matter what it took I would complete this program with flying colors. For the first time in years I was able to sense victory over my circumstances.

The only thing my reasoning could have provided would have been reaching the closest warm place to lay my head for the night but only to face doing it all over again the following day, eventually becoming even more lost on a road going nowhere. The following day while all the shelter brothers were preparing to leave the building to face their daily routine I was preparing for my first new day of the rest of my life. The days consisted of early morning praise and wordship followed by four biblical classes, two in the morning and two in the afternoon. I found the first class of the day to be my favorite. In this class from the bible we studied the gospel according to John which I found to be amazing.

What made it such was as we studied the scriptures it seemed as if the words from the pages were personally addressing my circumstance right down to the bare root of my struggle. It seemed unreal to experience the power and wisdom I was receiving from this book. It wasn't until we read Hebrews 4:12 which informs us that **the word of God is alive and active and sharper than any two-edged sword** that I began to understand what I was experiencing.

The word of God was working on me cutting through all the buildup mess in me breaking down the walls of pain, regret and confusion making room for the new man which was being build up. I believe God being true to his word means His word reflects the nature and character of who he is.

However we can find characters in the midst wherever we go. Not everyone there was there for the right reasons. Some were there just for a break from their madness while others like myself were there because they had nowhere else to go and in time we knew who those individuals were. I had noticed a chalkboard hanging by the front desk showing a list of names, these were names of those on restriction due to their disobedience to the rules. Being in a nine month program unable to interact with the outside world for the first four months being on the board was where I personally didn't want to be.

It meant anywhere from three to six days of no yard which is where we spent most of our free time when not watching restricted TV or sleeping . After 4PM till 8PM each weekday and mainly all weekend was our time. The yard provided weight training activities along with a basketball court and ping-pong table. The yard also served as our smoking area which was the only unrestricted area. I also noticed it seemed the same names were on the board week after week. One name I can't forget is O'Neal. From what I understood this was O'Neal's second or third go round. In his mid-twenties and the son of a preacher he was something else, defiant to the end.

I was baffled because I realized his knowledge of the bible surpassed most of the staff and interns. He had the knowledge in his head but denied it in his heart. I can only remember O'Neal as the one who got restriction while already on restriction. Remembering correctly it was also mentioned that he was mandated by the court to remain there until its completion which answered a lot because I also kept asking myself if he really didn't want to be there why not leave. He would interrupt classes just for the hell of it giving the pastor of the house, staff and intern fits. It was until he started attempting to interrupt the newcomer's by yelling through the building they were being brainwashed that they were forced to ask him to leave.

Having to report his removal from the premises it would only be a matter of time before O'Neal would be picked up by law enforcement for violating his court agreement. Sometimes I wonder what became of him and if he's alright. About three months into the program I was noticing as well as feeling a change in me. Life was beginning to look and feel different. I was feeling a little more confident in myself. In fact my favorite class required each of us read a scripture as we explored its meaning. In any other environment reading out loud would have been nerve racking because of my stumbling and stuttering. In what I know as a stressful situation I have a tendency to loss focus and train of thought and that's when I begin to breakdown.

From the first class even though I may have slightly stumbled I wasn't discouraged and it wasn't long before I welcomed reading and participating. Be the fourth month where many were calling themselves and work in progress I considered myself a miracle in progress. The more I learned, the more I wanted to know. I could feel the more of God's wisdom I absorbed the more I was also learning about myself. I was regaining my individuality, becoming my own person. I was in the beginning stages of an ongoing experience which was proving to be mind-blowing to say the least.

Used to living a life of expecting the worst as a shield against disappointment, now able to see myself in a new light I could also see victory in my grasped. God's word became my confirmation because there seemed to be scripture relating to everything I had and was experiencing in life. I found that after pondering over what I had read I could never dispute its wisdom. At the end of my fourth month I was given the option to stay in-house continuing classes, attending school or getting a job for the remaining months.

My first time out was with another guy going to a temporary job agency. Being right in the midst of my stumping ground so to speak I was well familiar with the environment but it was different now. Walking through I suddenly felt out of place like I didn't belong there. Furthermore, I began feeling as if they were sensing I didn't belong there and being there gave me an eerie feeling.

As I said, this was a mind-blowing experience and that's the only way I know to describe it. We reached our destination but nothing good happened. The rule was if we weren't sent out to work too come back to the house. Out there just lingering around wasn't the way to go but instead this guy wanted to hang out by a busy downtown bus stop just to be out there as if something out there he was missing.

Out for the first time had me in an uncomforting state of being but one returning without the other for me also wasn't the way to go, so after seeing I wasn't having it we finally headed back. On my way out a few days later to a different agency telling one of the interns where I was headed, I never forgot his response which also sent me in a different direction. He said, "God didn't save you to work in a warehouse" which led me to set my goal higher. After looking into it the program helped me get into a non-profit state run school where I was able to learn computer applications like Microsoft word, excel and so on.

Mind you, I was and still is a miracle in progress so sometimes old habits may still flair up now and again. I was starting a computer course and one of the qualifications was having a high school diploma. Even knowing ahead for some reason on the application and interview when asked if I had a diploma I answered yes both times. A week through the course I'm hoping they forget but now the instructor's asking me. I know for a fact the old me would have caved in, packed up and moved on with a defeated mind-set.

All though I knew I had messed up and maybe even beyond repair I still felt this was the direction I should be going. I decided I had to rise above the false-pride, fear and embarrassment of my actions, walk into the case-worker's office, sat down and explain myself to the best of my ability and hope for the best. After the conversation the case-worker agreed if I started working on my diploma right away they would hold my spot for six months. So far it was better than I had hoped for. It took me about a week before attending GED classes three hours a day five days a week.

Now I think is a good time to share the answer to the earlier question, why of all places this area. After four months we were able to apply for weekend passes for the day or weekend. It was also preferred that those who could afford it to be responsible for their own laundry by using outside laundry-mats. Now, I not only regularly brought my drugs from this area, for about a year previous to Hackensack I lived in this area, so I pretty much knew the lay of the land. I also knew the closet laundry-mat was about a block from where I lived and also right in the midst of it all, petty thugs, dealers, addicts, cheap hookers, cocaine, heroin or crack. An area where it seemed everybody was on something.

It was a Saturday morning when I needed to wash clothes. On my way to the laundry-mat I didn't pay much attention to what was going on around me, just on my way. Reaching the laundry-mat and getting the washers rolling I decided to step out in front and have a smoke. As I stood right across the street from where I brought my drugs observing it was as if seeing through different eyes. All I could see was their pain, confusion and hopelessness. I watched as the late night and early morning scramblers moved to and fro going nowhere. The longer I observed the more I began to realize I was observing myself.

I was seeing the pain, regret, and hopelessness their eyes reflected, the same pain, regret and hopelessness I carried inwardly and my eyes reflected outwardly. I began thinking, this use to be me. Months ago I was trapped in a madness cycle not knowing if I was coming or going and many times not even caring. I recalled hating my life and myself for what I had become because at the end of it all I had no one to blame but myself. Then it hit me, this place for this moment, to reveal firsthand the fullness of where He had brought me from. For the first time in twenty plus years I knew with all confidence I was no longer that person.

2Corinthians 5:17 confirms it this way: *Therefore, if anyone is in Christ he is a new creation, old things have passed away behold, all things are new.* God through Christ was making it possible for me to be a living witness to His existence, His lifesaving and life changing power. God was at work doing a new thing in me and it couldn't be denied.

I was spiritually in a zone riding high because I was able to rise each morning, look in the mirror proudly at the person looking back. I knew I looked and felt healthier than I had in years but more so inside where change is most important I had never experienced anything like it. Manmade organizations told me I would always be what I was, once an addict always an addict. I always felt following that philosophy was only setting yourself up for failure.

They told me I would have to learn to deal with a lifetime struggle of sobriety. I use to sit in on N/A meetings where guys with years of sobriety would be sitting in front of the room behind a long table giving their testimony. They all proclaimed their lives were better and happier but observing while listening they just didn't seem like happy individuals, as if for whatever reason they weren't at peace with themselves.

The word of God told me I was a new creation, old things had passed away and all things were new. I already knew that when my time to leave came I wouldn't have to confront any doubt because my past had no place in my present or future. I was learning that when we take man's advice we get man's results but when we take God's advice we get the best results.

I hadn't been inside a classroom close to thirty years and now I was back learning math, English and whatever else it took over again to earn my GED. The class was a nice size with mixed nationality and ages. Some attending were sharing their negative hear-says saying many fail their first time. All the while I'm thinking I'm on a time schedule, I can't afford to fail. During this time my nine month graduation from the Mission was quickly approaching.

I reflected over my time there, I arrived about 145lbs with three pairs of pants, three shirts, three pairs of underwear and what I had on. I was homeless, lost and alone. I had been a functioning addict for most of my life until I became a broken hopeless addict who had finally reached the point of seeing suicide as his only way of having freedom from the hell I allowed to take root within me. I was leaving about 175lbs looking good and feeling great with a full wardrobe.

I was feeling more confident in myself than I had ever felt, I knew nothing within me was or would ever be the same. Still I felt that nervous energy realizing I was on my way out to face the outside would once again.

For the first time I didn't have any fear or doubt of keeping the course, I knew of the dangers out there, the Good Shepherd Mission had been my safe haven the past nine months. Now preparing to leave my safe place for good left me with mixed feelings but I also knew it was time. I had witnessed brothers become stuck there. This wasn't the type of place that would push you out when your time there was up, they'd tell us if we felt we weren't ready we could stay longer.

Some stayed becoming interns and then live-in staff members, some for legitimate reasons but most out of fear of leaving their safe place. The staff member that led me from seeking a warehouse job to going to school was a resident five year prior. During his five year stay he had become a very good teacher as well as staff member but I believe his main reason for staying is he didn't believe he could stay strong on the outside. It wasn't the past crack addiction that kept him there, it was the war within concerning his sexual preference.

After six years he finally decided to step out of his comfort zone. I asked about him a year later and the news was he had a nervous breakdown. I can only imagine what caused it. Being in the Mission was the best thing that had ever happened to me and I was leery about leaving but I felt with every fiber of my being that God had more in store for me but in order to receive it I had to put my trust in Him and step out on faith. Wanting all that God had to offer I did just that. It's been over twenty years and still so grateful for the time I spent in the Mission I still have my certificate proudly hanging on my living-room wall. I will always view the Good Shepherd Mission as the place where life for me began.

CERTIFICATE OF

In Appreciation

THIS CERTIFIES THAT

Steven Sima

HAS BEEN RECOGNIZED

FOR completion of the French program

BY the Good Shepherd Mission

ON THE 22nd DAY OF December IN THE YEAR OF OUR LORD 1999 Rev Michael V.

"LET YOUR LIGHT SO SHINE BEFORE MEN.
THAT THEY MAY SEE YOUR GOOD WORKS.
AND GLORIFY YOUR FATHER WHICH IS IN HEAVEN."

While in the Mission I had no idea Joyce was expecting us to work things out between us because I hadn't heard from her since dropping me off. While on a daily pass and running into an old friend something began rekindling and we both decided to play it by ear. After graduation I moved in with her and her eleven year old daughter. I was still attending GED classes and soon I would also be working a part time job in the seafood department of the neighborhood supermarket.

This was truly a new me and I was loving it. I was on the move having no idea what the future held but it looked bright, for the first time I felt nothing but good things waiting over the horizon. I'm not sure how Joyce got the number to my work place or even where I worked. I got on the phone and she said she wanted us to talk ASAP. I figured it would be a good time to clear up any confusion so I told her when my next break was. When I got outside she was already there parked. We greeted each other and then I began explaining that for my own well-being I couldn't return back there, whatever was behind had to stay behind.

It was time for me to move forward. She began crying and I began apologizing while telling her it was just the way it had to be. Suddenly her demeanor changed as she began asking repeatedly, well what about me? I had no answer for that, all I knew was I couldn't go backwards. I saw her months later during a church service I attended in Hackensack and she rolled her eyes at me so I thought it better not to approach her. I did kind of look for her after the service but she had disappeared, it was curiosity that's all.

The old me wouldn't have been able to have that conversation. I was weak like that, I'd rather just sneak off and put it all out of my mind. Mainly because I've always been sensitive to a woman's emotions. Even in my mess I never wanted to be the type of man that caused pain. However that's the person I had become, never physical but many times emotional pain can do just as much damage to a person's well-being. I didn't like dealing with emotional issues and crying was the worst because it was heartbreaking for me, especially if I caused it. Why go through that if I didn't have to. But things had changed, this new man had given birth to new strength and wisdom to facie consequences and responsibilities.

Running, hiding, avoiding was no longer an option, whether I was reluctant to or not the only option in moving forward. At forty-five years old I actually felt like I was growing up all over again and it felt weird in a good way. I was experiencing a pos-itive change in me while living a life I was genuinely enjoying without the reliance of drugs as a mood adjuster or confidence building, just me on a nat-ural high. Where I once only seen darkness ahead, no purpose or direction, now I saw possibility.

I had a confidence in myself I'd never experi-enced before. I hadn't reached my purpose yet but I had direction and a focus on that direction. The GED test came up in five instead of six months but I was still able to take it and I passed by one point. The funny part is in reaching the time limit the front and back of the last three or four pages I just checked boxes so all the questions would be answered. After receiving the news of passing with all things considered I knew I was back on track.

A week later I was back in class learning computer applications. Old things were passing away, all things were becoming new. I know many would rather believe and say I just finally grew up rather than believe in a God that can supernaturally intervene on our behalf. However I myself don't know of anyone who has been dependently embracing drugs for over twenty years and just made a 360 degree turn. Changing habits is one thing but still displaying addict characteristics is not a 360, the heart and mentality must also change.

After twenty-five years of drugging one of life's many harsh realities I believe true is that change of the heart and mind can only be achieved from inside out. Twenty-five years of drugging half of which became out of my control bringing alone with it suffering. After those many years there is always remaining residue which can take years to dissolve. All I'm saying is it was a process taking years getting from where I started to where I ended up and it took less than a year of leaving the Mission to experience surpassing any expectations I might have had.

Experiencing this continuing change in me was still hard to wrap my head around and it was only the beginning. While attending computer classes I was still working the part-time job at the supermarket. They offered me more hours and a manger position but I knew that wasn't my destination, just a stepping stone. Once I finished the course I had no idea where it would lead but I knew I would be moving on. I figured I'd go the route that's always been reliable, the temporary agencies. I would usually sign up with at least two agencies to better my chances.

With a little more office skills under my belt I'd find a cozy office position which is the environment I felt I belonged. I was believing everything would fall together. In fact it seemed everything had been falling so much into place and beyond I began believing all the bad was behind me and it would continue to be smooth sailing from now on. Oh boy did I find that thought to be misleading. Trials and tribulations unfortunately go with the territory because we have an enemy whose mission is to steel, kill and destroy.

Steel our joy, hopes and dreams, **kill** the spirit and what's left is a dead man walking, the spirit and **destroy** any hope of ever recovering, this is the battle we face daily. I'm reminded of the military how during orientation period it's calm and pleasant as we're receiving our gear and instructions while being introduced us to the environment. During that time if you don't know any better it's easy to believe it's going to remain that way. We don't expect the drastic change about to take place, a change that has brought many to tears but at the end reveals what we're made of.

I was about to step into my first test as a new man. When I first moved in with Penny my now wife the transition wasn't as smooth as it could have been. I stepped into an arena to soon and unprepared. A mother of two daughters, the oldest was out of the home not of her own choosing while the other an eleven year old was still living at home. The same night of moving in I fall witness to a heated verbal dispute and although invited into that conflict by the mother, at such an early stage while not knowing much about nothing I should have stayed back and let it play itself out.

Not doing so created a rocky beginning but not long afterwards the waves seemed to calm and things seemed to be coming together. It was the calm before the storm. The relationship between my wife's daughter and I was good as far as I could tell but the more she grew into her teens the more shaky the relationship became. Penny would put me in positions where I was forced as a husband to reinforce her role as a parent. The daughter not used to discipline especially from someone she still viewed as an outsider she began seeing me as a threat to her home life. I could see she had her mother just where she wanted her.

As discipline Penny would yell and curse until she was all worked up and then things went back to normal but without truly addressing or solving anything. I come in with new rules like punishment without TV, cell phone or any other type of entertainment, I would tell her if she want entertainment read a book. Soon she began fighting back telling me to take all the entertainment from her room, she didn't care if she never got them back. The longer I remained the more hostile the environment became, now she was disrespecting both of us because she knew the law as it is today was on her side regardless of the circumstances.

She would even try baiting me by calling me out my name while daring me to hit her but she needed a more updated playbook for that to work. Many times I'd find myself brought down to her level in a yelling match that only frustrated me. Some of the daughter's friends liked and respected my wife and would come back telling what she would be saying. She'd express how much she hated me and that her mission was to break up our relationship so things could go back to the way it was, in other words when she could have her way without anyone in her way.

Penny with more bark than bite would never do what she was supposed to. Sometimes I would wish I could just draw back one time and slap the taste out of her mouth but without the consequences, wishful thinking. Still today the youngest daughter and I respect and tolerate each other but neither under any circumstances can we reside under the same roof. Besides what you've already read there's an isolated reason for my decision. I mentioned about stepping into my first test as a new man, well this is about coming close to failing but in order to share it I have to bring us to closer to present time.

But I think it's appropriate for this time and maintains the flow of the book. We can look at our life and know without doubt the favor of God shines on us daily nevertheless trouble doesn't rest and never ceases to creep in from time to time. About three years ago the younger daughter needed a place to stay for a couple months. Penny is full of that mother's love, the kind where a mother can be treated like dirt by her children and the following couple days act as if nothing ever happened.

Knowing we had the extra room that was once hers now my man-cave she asked Penny if she could stay with us. Even knowing what my answer would be instead of answering on my behalf she'd rather come and ask me so I'd be the bad guy. So she asked and I answered and she goes back to the phone. Now she comes back with this pleading look on her face telling me about the weather, how it's only for a couple months and how she didn't want to see her daughter out in the cold with nowhere to go. I just threw my hands up and blurted out in frustration, I don't care what you do.

The next thing I knew the daughter's walking in the door with her bags, here to seize my man-cave. I already knew how things were going to go but Penny kept insisting she had changed, how she was older and wiser now but I knew better. Sure enough that nasty disrespectful person began emerging and all hell began to break loose. We said nobody spends the night and her girlfriend comes on visits and then spending nights. Penny knowing the already tension between us would ask me to not say anything.

In order to keep the peace for her sake I would hold my tongue but us clashing was unavoidable because that's how thick the tension was. When it happened it was as ugly and uncomfortable as I knew it would be because I knew I had too much to lose to allow myself to get caught up in the non-sense. It was now a month past the two month mark and a couple confrontations had already taken place, all the while I wouldn't let Penny forget this was all her fault. My answer was no for both of our good and she knew that but still allowed her daughter who has no problem jumping up in her face cursing her out to convince her to not just override me but her own common-sense.

My next decision even caught me by surprise. I decided I'd had enough and that it was time for her to clean up her own mess. I told Penny I was leaving and wasn't coming back until her daughter was gone and that's what I did for three months. I let Penny deal with her daughter on her own and it nearly led to a nervous breakdown or worse. I knew if I went out and rented a place I might not come back and that wasn't my intention.

I knew she wouldn't be able to handle the pressure but my thought was she brought it on herself so deal with it. I know you're wondering where I went for three months. I back to the mission, the place where I was transformed into someone I liked a lot. I'm sorry I had to lie and tell them I had a problem which I did, it just wasn't a drug problem. Penny would come every visit no matter what the weather.

With each visit I could see a little more wear and tear, a couple visits I could tell she wanted to break down and it hurt seeing her that way but I kept telling myself she brought it on herself.

It wasn't the first time, she has a habit of taking others advice over mine, even when hearing the same advice she'll come back saying this one or that one told me I should do this. At the end of three months which make six months the daughter has been there Penny came to visit me looking as if her strength was nearly gone. She began telling me her daughter probably thinking I'm gone for good was refusing to leave. Under some New Jersey law if a person has been staying with you longer than six months you caught just put them out, you have to go through the legal system.

She was hurt to see her daughter would throw this law in her face and go through such extremes but I wasn't surprised one bit. That day I felt so bad for her I asked if she wanted me to come home and her face lite up with relief. We left together that evening and when we walked through the door the shocked expression on the daughter's face was priceless. About a half hour later Penny was in the kitchen standing over the sink. I'm not sure what words were passed but I think the shock of seeing me hit such a sensitive nerve her outburst couldn't be contained.

The next thing I knew the daughter was rushing in on Penny in such a threatening manner I seen the fear in her eyes as she called out for me. Without saying a word I walked up and stepped between them and then came the baiting, "and what you gonna do, you gonna hit me, go ahead I dare you. Still never saying a word she's began calling me all the gay slurs she could think of but she's guy. To wrap this up we went to court and the daughter tried pleading a case she never had in spite of that law.

The judge gave her thirty days to be out which Penny and I thought was to long but knowing we had to go along we started the count down from day one. There was a time when in situations like this I wouldn't have hesitated to pack my little belongings and be on my way for good but I had made a promise to God beforehand there would be no more running because that had always been my way of solving problems.

I thank God I was able to stay the course. Even leaving for those three months I believe was all in his plan. Of all places just look at where I thought to go, a place where I wouldn't be swayed from a plan in motion, it was something I had to do to maintain my sanity. Having to control one's self in such chaotic circumstances is not an easy task. Also my wife fighting against her husband's wishes allowing chaos to enter our home had to be addressed so that this would never happen again. She had to gain a comprehension of the damage she had caused. Today I look back at the many blessings I would have missed out on if I had not stayed the course.

But no matter how blessed we are Every day is not going to be sunny, storms, sometimes terrible storms will come but how we chose to confront the storm is what makes all the difference in the course our life takes. I was no longer that person who avoided and had no desire to be, I now chose to confront but wisely. When I'd reached my forties I believed I had wasted all my chances because I'd been given so many. Here, I wasn't just given another chance, I was given a new life and I was planning to take full advantage whatever it took. In spite of the turmoil I was facing I also knew with Penny is where I was supposed to be.

But even though I knew it everything around me was trying to convince me I'd made a bad choice. Family members hers and mine were shocked in disbelief because Penny was considered the least irrelevant according to their standards. Although she may not have been able to see I seen it and it would upset me seeing her upset, but I'd hold my tongue because that was their relationship. I could see they all loved her but they would also sometimes lovingly as they call it tease her usually at family gatherings, and I hated that.

Penny is the type of person you can't help but love because in spite of her flaws she has a heart full of love and compassion. I was told I made a mistake, I need to have the marriage annulled or I could do better. I see how blessed Penny and I am today and I think what if I would have listened to the many voices instead of the main voice which led me here. Where would I be today, would I be the man I am today, would I be as content and at peace with my life as I am today, somehow I just don't think so.

What's funny is Penny and I as a family have been able in one way or other to be a blessing to all who in the beginning opposed this union.

Today many view my wife who they know years before as not just a family member but a reliable and trusting friend which didn't manifest until after our union. Without even trying that's how things work when we're where we should be in life. Before coming together neither one of us could have ever imagined living a life of such peace and contentment. What God had joined together let no one come between.

The temporary job agency sent me on assignment to an Italian clothing firm helping in the office. After working there a year I was offered a position in their order entry department. Life was great, like at AT&T I was wearing a shirt and tie everyday which was big for me. That's how I always pictured myself at work, in a shirt and tie behind a desk and now equipped with a new mentality I was able to learn, enjoy as well as appreciate the experience.

I was working for a clothing firm I never heard of but well-known by the rich and famous. I was feeling real good about myself, coming from where I'd been you could say I was feeling on top of the world.

Because of my pleasant disposition I was already well accepted throughout the office. I was making a good salary with benefits and perks that would take my life and focus to a whole new level. The kind of company that had annual cookouts and rented clubs spaces in New York to host our Christmas parties which included transportation. I was seeing the strides I was making, experiencing a growth process and as I was taking it all in I know I was truly still a work, a miracle in progress.

I'd always believed my childhood played a big part of my wandering in darkness. How I was made to feel about myself I believe was the primary reason for choosing a dark path, I was unable to see any good in me. It was 2003, two years into being employed when out of nowhere came an idea to write a book. I didn't know the first thing about it, in fact the idea had never even crossed my mind until this moment. Even in conversation I've never had much to say, finding enough to say for a book was impossible.

A whispering voice within revealed that this was part of my healing process, in order to continue forward in my spiritual growth I had to first grow beyond my past. Like I said, I knew nothing about writing, I'm thinking to myself, this must be wishful thinking I never knew I had, I not too long ago just got my GED, you need writing skills to write, I don't have that. It'll probably take about five years just to come up with enough to say.

After going back and forward with myself I sat down in front of the computer trying to figure out how to begin, what do I say, do I start with hello, by introducing myself, what the hell do I do? One Sunday morning I was listening to a TV preacher, I can't say what the sermon was about. What I do remember was him mentioning us all having a need to belong and it hit me, as a child I always had the need of belonging, a need that was never fulfilled or even recognized.

From that point I just began typing what was coming to mind while trying to put it together so it made sense. It was definitely a challenge. I began noticing the more I began loosening up the more painful memories that came to mind and the more I just wanted to sat in front of the computer screen typing it in.

After a while once the number of pages began accumulating I began getting impatient towards publishing. Me of all people, I couldn't have never imagined an accomplishment like this, this was way out of my league. Looking at all the evidence I knew it was no body but God, call me naïve, I find it just too hard to believe this was just my idea.

In 2005 the self-published book, A Desire to Belong / Breaking Free was published. I realized when it was too late that the book was nowhere ready for publication. For one thing I didn't get the focus it needed, it's one thing having soft easy listening music on. This time around I found it helps the flow of thought. It's a whole other thing when you have the TV on next to you, now you focus is divided and that was me then. This cause the book to be full of typos and no real flow but at that time it looked good to me, it was full of pages.

Becoming overwhelmed by the thought of a published book with my name on it as author overrode patience and common sense. After the deed was done I found myself unable to put any effort behind advertising because of my lack of satisfaction with the work I had done. I sold a few copies but knowing the book was being read made me feel like most artist who paint. They never want anyone to see their work before its completion, I really didn't want anyone to read the book because I felt it was incomplete. It would be sixteen years before God would guide me to rectify my misjudgment.

I've found that most of the storms we face in life we bring on ourselves. It was a nice summer evening I had just gotten off work. The only thing from my past that I still struggle with is cigarettes however it's not all I do. I also smoke marijuana, why? Because I enjoy it. Yes I am a child of God but I'm not a saint. I believe anything that causes us to act out of nature, other than who God created us to be should have no place in our life, and that includes alcohol. I doubt if anyone could recall any terrible incident or crime where marijuana was the cause.

This was 2005 long before it became legal, while I was changing my clothes I was smoking a joint and decided to smoke the other half in the park across the street.

I had been there maybe twenty minutes and re-lighting the joint for the third time a plan car rolled up on me and a cop stepped out. By this time the joint is not much longer than a regular match. He said because I was also fifty feet from a school which was closed for the day I was handcuffed and taken to the station. He was mentioning writing me a summons and releasing me and right then I'm thinking he could have done that back there.

A few minutes later he comes back telling me he had some bad news. They found seven outstanding warrants pending from four different counties. It felt as if my heart had dropped to my stomach, the news triggered flashbacks. I remembered when life was dark and I had nothing to lose situations like this would just roll off my back. But this was not the case. What had I done? I'd come too far to get knocked back now. I had too much to lose. However I was also aware of past consequences that hadn't been addressed but after ten years the thought became dormant, but I never imagined it would be so bad, one or two but seven.

I began thinking about losing my job and having to start all over, and I would never land another job like this. Once again I had no one to blame but myself. I'd made it a habit to smoke inside as it should have been at that time but that day I chose to go outside because the weather was nice. I allowed stupidity to override my common sense. Sometimes things can be going so smooth we tend to get to relaxed and that's when we usually make unwise choices.

We let our guard down allowing our common sense to be overshadowed. Before being moved to a different county under a dark cloud and at a lost I called Penny and gave her the bad news. Viewing the situation after the fact I can now see God's wakeup call in action, but not only for concern in getting too relaxed. God never does anything half way, he knew I couldn't continue moving forward with unaddressed consequences of my past hanging over my head. The one thing God doesn't remove is consequences but He's always been a present help in my time of need. Meanwhile Penny was at work with only one thought in mind, getting her husband home. We had become good friends with a young woman I worked with named Tawanda.

Adopting me as her big brother because I was her parent's age she'd invite us to family cookouts and other gathers. Crazy about Penny she would come pick her up just to ride around, hang out in stores or whatever, for some reason being the first person who came to mind Penny called Tawanda. I don't know how they did it, all I know is the two put their heads together and worked magic.

Meanwhile I had reached the county jail spending all night in a holding cell being processed. At this point I had no expectations of getting out any time soon. Focused on the worst scenario I figured by the time all this was over I'd be back to square one, out of a job living in uncertainty, most likely ending up back working with temp agencies. I was beating myself up because at a time when even though I felt I didn't deserve it I was given another chance, possibly my last and now that was gone, and it didn't have to be.

I was hurt and upset and although I believed the journey wasn't over I also believed it would never be the same. It was the next morning and all I wanted to do was reach a final destination with a bed. That same morning Tawanda and my wife went to the job and into human resources. One of the perks was a 401k investment plan. During those five years I had accumulated enough funds to borrow from. Usually it would take at least forty-eight hours to receive your loan but those two were able to concoct whatever story and get the paperwork that morning.

They brought the paperwork to the jail, had the officer bring me out to sign them and had $10,000 in my checking account by twelve mid-night. I had gotten assigned my ceil, walking in and about to lay down on my nice clean sheets when they called my name for release. After trying to find comfort on a hard cement floor all night I was so tired and that bed was looking so good I almost didn't want to go right then. When I was finally released an hour later the whole gang was sitting in the car waiting patiently, Tawanda and Penny sitting in the front with Tawanda's new husband knocked out sleep in the back.

I was back home in my own bed by 2am and back to work the following day. For the next two or three months I made seven different court appearances paying a total of seven thousand dollars in fines. Walking into each courtroom facing outstanding warrants the judges weren't trying to hear anything except, "yes I have your money", anything else was a waste of time. I contribute this outcome to doing things God's way, allowing him to guide my path. I learned that lesson from that cold winter evening when he led me out of the darkest days of my life.

Like never before I found myself prepared for what was to come which confirmed in my spirit that even in my errors I was doing something right and the favor of God still remained on me. God already know we're going to screw up because it's in our nature for one. Also He know the beginning and ending of our story, he just doesn't interfere unless we invite him in. I believe the two things God truly requires of us is first to get to know him and secondly that we stride be the best of who we are.

The person He created which is the best of who we are is automatically mindful of how we interact and treat each other. Being the best of who we are gives us the power to regulate our thoughts and actions. Our responsibility requires us to stride to be the best of who we be, not the best of what we see. After the court incident I remained working for the same company for the following four years until the recession hit in 2008. By the middle of 2009 almost half the office personnel were let go including myself after nine years.

As compensation I was let go in July but continued to receive a weekly paycheck until the end of the year plus collect full unemployment the same time. To top it off was my 401k so I guess you could say I wasn't to upset about suddenly being unemployed. Life was great, for the time being I didn't have to worry about much of anything. Things were good before but now, a person could get used to just sitting at home collecting a weekly hefty pay. I never received severance pay before and just think, twelve years prior I could have never imagined myself in such a position.

At the time there were no jobs and most were forced to rely solely on unemployment but we was blessed even during such an uneasy time for most. During this time through the help of my wife I picked up a hobby. Penny noticed how interested I was in this TV art program. It was a white guy with an afro painting on canvas. I was always amazed how in a half hour from a blank canvas he could create such beautiful landscape scenes. He would talk while painting telling the viewers the colors and techniques used and I would think to myself, I could never do that. If it would have remained left up to me I'd still be convincing myself I could never do it.

As a Christmas gift Penny went out and purchased everything needed to start my venture and I've been at it ever since. At first it became discouraging because a brushes to paint a house sure I had never picked up this type of brush in my life. As a kid I drew cartoon characters but what child hasn't, this was a whole different level and I was no longer a kid. But as I continued following the manuals with patients and time I began seeing progress. Soon it became something I truly enjoyed, creating. Imagine starting out with a blank canvas and a vision already knowing along the way the vision may be altered.

Nevertheless you work through it possibly having to take an alternate route but you see it coming together. To complete your work and then step back to admire what you've done every time is a reward in itself. I pride myself on being self-taught because I had convinced myself I couldn't do it. To achieve it on my own confirms I almost fully missed out on a talent that's always been a part of me but never utilized. I paint for the love of it, I've sold a few from time to time from home as well as street fairs.

I've given many away because everything I have is a blessing from God so whenever possible I enjoy being a blessing. Being an African American I've been asked by other African Americans why have I not done any black art. Because my paintings don't embrace just the black culture even though painted by a black man it's not considered black art?

I know what they're asking but I consider my work as universal embracing all cultures because we all can see some of God's actual handy-work and be left in amazement. For those like myself who don't travel much, whatever nationality we enjoy seeing paintings and photos of God's handy-work, it's universal.

The main reason I love landscape scenes is because of the peaceful spirit within me therefore I love creating scenes of tranquility. Daily we deal with the drama and craziness of life, I try to reflect the tranquil side of life. To me there is nothing more beautiful or peaceful then God's earthly creativity unblemished by man. What I do doesn't give the beauty of His creation the justice due but it brings satisfaction knowing what I create reflects the spirit he has placed within me.

For the first five months of being laid off it felt as if money was just flowing in. We already had an abundance of all we needed and wanted, now Penny found the need to start buying an overabundance of everything like we were preparing for a famine. Sometimes we could hardly find room for everything but she always had a full meal for anybody who wanted one. I could go looking for something I seen earlier to eat but by the time I get to it she be done gave it away.

She would see people she knew while looking out the window asking them if they needed anything like we were running a food pantry. At times I'd get a little upset but that was on me. After reminding myself of who we were and realizing it was all coming from her heart it was all good. Why be stingy if you have more than enough. Sometimes I have to put myself in check by reminding myself of who I am and who I represent.

However, I am who I am. Romans 3:23 tells us for all have sinned and fall short of the glory of God. Notice what it doesn't say, all have sinned and fallen. 3:10 tell us there is none righteous, not even one. Fall in the present tense suggest that we constantly fall short. No matter how much we say we love God and live to please him we can't help what's in our nature, that's why we have the responsibility of keeping ourselves in check by the wisdom of His word.

It had been a while since having so much free time on my hands. Soon I'd allow my mind to wandering down the dark corridors of the past. This is when our minds begin to reflect back skipping over the bad times to reflect the good. The bible teaches that Satan attacks the minds by distorting our thinking. Left unchecked it could lead us where we know we shouldn't be. For reasons unknown, maybe it was boredom, maybe it was the money, maybe it was both that caused me to leave my misguide thoughts unchecked.

Out walking one day I happen to run into a brother I knew was still getting high. We stopped and talked for a few and then he asked for ten dollars. I automatically knew what he wanted it for so I inquired a little more. I knew wherever he had to go it wasn't far.

My reasoning suddenly became "a dime or twenty is not going to hurt anything" It had been over ten years and now here I was once again testing the waters. The more I loosened up the more money I was spending. Before long I was venturing back over to the old familiar territory not far from the Mission. I began coming in all hours of the night, sometimes with crack and a stem in my pocket. I would go into my back room, close the door while sneaking to finish what was left. I remember the nights of just foolishly wasting money because getting high while enjoying the added perks was my main objective.

Unlike the past knowing I didn't have to worry about running out of money while out there made me act even more of a fool. This went on about a month before coming to my senses or maybe because the funds was beginning to run low. I'm not going to say I put myself in check because if that was the case I wouldn't have been out there in the first place. Honestly, I just got tired. I was disrespecting my wife and our home as well as myself. Not only that, it wasn't the same because I had experienced another life, a better life and I knew it was above this life. I loved my life so why was I even here.

I knew better, I was well aware of the dangers I was opening myself up to and still I gave into the misguided thoughts. Once Satan had persuaded us to follow his lead we who are no longer his puppets must always be alert. Even though he may no longer have a foothold in our life his mission to steal, kill and destroy doesn't change. Every person he loses means a failed mission but Satan doesn't accept defeat therefore he's won't just move on. He's constantly plotting ways to get us back to where it thinks we belong but under Satan's foot is not where any of us belong.

I became a victim due to lack of knowledge. The more I discovered about God through his word the more I seemed to also discovery about myself. Satan doesn't want that because once we become aware his power is diminished. Our belief in the knowledge we've been given strengthens, sharpens and guides our awareness. Today I'm able to be victorious in life but then it depends on how you define victorious.

Having the finest things in life is great, having more money than we need is very good but if we don't have the genuine love, peace, joy, and content- ment that flows from within can we really enjoy life?

Living a victorious life is not defined be what we own or by the titles we hold. We've seen many who seemed to be living their dreams becoming able to afford whatever they desire but finding themselves entangled in the stupidest circumstances costing them nearly if not everything.

We hear or read about it and unable to understand we have to ask ourselves, why? It doesn't make sense. A simple answer is because they were still dissatisfied with their life. With all that they'd accumulated there was still something missing and when we don't know what we're looking for we'll always find ourselves looking in all the wrong places. So the question was if we don't have the genuine love, peace, joy, and contentment that flows from within can we really enjoy life?

As my unemployment began drawing closer to an end I knew it was time to hit the bricks job hunting. Temporary agencies always being my first choice without hesitation I made appointments with two out of town. I found long ago that out of town agencies offered better assignments with better wages, you just had to be willing to travel to out of town locations. As time drew nearer I began getting nervous. The recession was passing over and jobs were beginning to reopen. My mean concern was job competition and opportunities for a black male in his late fifties with no real solid skills.

I had sat back for nearly three years living off my combining severance pay, unemployment and 401k now with only a couple thousand dollars in between my last unemployment check which was three weeks away and my first paycheck. Time was long past due for facing reality, for a short time I may have forgotten I was still a member of the working class with bills to pay. In a few days I received a call from one of the agencies wanting me to come in for an interview.

Most of the more upscale agencies required interviews but they were nothing like interviewing with the actual company where they ask questions seemingly trying to trip you up. All the agencies were concerned with was if we were able to fulfill the job requirements. I didn't drive so I always kept bus fare handy. The day before the interview I went online and mapped out the bus route and time, being late for an interview in the interviewer's eyes is a sign the person is neither serious nor reliable.

Arriving in the immediate location of the agency with forty-five minutes to spare I began looking for the building but for some reason I just couldn't find it. At one time I went into what I thought was the correct building but when searching the directory the agency name was nowhere to be found. However I did see another agency I was unfamiliar with. With still time to spare I exited the building deciding to search once more. Coming up short again I decide to try the agency I had seen on the building directory.

After arriving and filling out an application I was asked to have a seat. A few minutes later a woman led me to her office, she asked a few questions and the said, you came in just in time, we just brought in a new client and I think you'll be just right for the position. She said she was on her way to meet with then once the interview was over and I should receive a call later that evening or the following day. That was on a Wednesday and the following Monday I was on my way to work. God was still at work, I knew it because I'm always looking at the evidence.

I went looking for an agency I never could find but because I was determined I ran across a different agency. Deciding to take a chance I went inside and then hearing the words the woman spoke to me, it seemed as if this venture was tailored just for me. Once arriving at the jobsite it felt even more so. It was a small dental company which employed twelve warehouse workers but generated over two million dollars a month. The pay wasn't bad with a raise every year, 401k plan and decent insurance. However we all would laugh because we found it funny that a dental supply company didn't provide dental insurance.

I found it refreshing to find the majority of the employees were in my age range and seemed family oriented joking and laughing while at work including the supervisor. The coworkers began telling me I would find this to be the easiest warehouse job I'd ever worked and they weren't lying. Most products were less than two pound, no single cases over twenty-five pounds. The company's main concern was making sure the orders were shipped correctly. In order for such a small company to clock over two million dollars a month things have to move quickly.

After working for six months as a temporary employee I was offered a full time position. Working in the receiving department becoming the only stock person my main responsibility was making sure the correct products were stocked in the right locations. Pickers move quickly pushing their cart picking and logging each item and location picked from.

Sometimes moving fast to get a shipment out they may not examine every item because they know what's supposed to be in that location. So if something is shipped incorrectly and they go back to the log-sheet to find the wrong product was picked from an incorrect location now I'm implicated along with the picker and the packer who's also the shipper.

This company also had its little perks in effort to show its appreciation like annual cookouts and Christmas bonuses which they gave out at the Christmas parties held at rented establishments. What I enjoyed was the once a week variety of bagels and muffins with the dressings they'd have brought in. By the end of the day there was enough left over for some employees to take home. I worked for the company about six years before being laid off due to the pandemic.

I believe God was preparing me for this time. He is the beginning and the end knowing our choices and actions before we do but as I said earlier He doesn't directly interfere. However when we are sensitive to his presence in our life he's able to navigate us through the rough waters that are to surely come whether by our own making or circumstances beyond our control.

I was months from my sixty-fifth birthday when the pandemic hit and people were considerably being laid off. I wasn't worried as far as the job because I was planning on retiring and collecting my social security at sixty-five anyway. There was a time I didn't think I would make it to be old enough to retire and now that I was nearly there I wasn't wasting any time. I quickly filed for my unemployment and then straight to the social security office.

I had picked up a few pointers concerning the filing process from the older brother I was working with. Preparing for retirement before the pandemic he'd already gone through the process. What I thought was going to be a difficult drawn out process turned to be fairly simple and I was very pleased because when it comes to something that's essential I hate difficulty. Experiencing going through the scariest scenario this country, the world has ever faced in our lifetime I discovered a part of me I'd never witnessed before.

I'd poisoned my body for years with so many different street drugs and seen so many because of the abuse here but gone, the body's still here but the spirit and mind never recovered. To witness myself navigate through what was and still is a stressful time for most I felt real good about myself. I found myself always trying to think ahead especially after witnessing my wife' spending habits. We were both able to collect unemployment plus we both collected a monthly check which combined was enough to maintain all the comforts of home.

Once the stimulus money began that's when the spending began. Penny discovered she could have stuff delivered by shopping online. The one thing I learned about her early on was that she's loved spending money, she just didn't have none to spend. Now with what seemed to her like extra money she could sat back in the comfort of her own home searching the web for stuff to buy. I would go online and order my paints and supplies and because she was now home all day paying more attention to me and my hobby, now she wanted a hobby to. She began telling me of her back in the day crocheting.

Soon she was online ordering the tools of her reborn hobby. It seemed like every couple days she was ordering more yearn preparing for a new project. Things were going well for a good while. She was calling family members asking their favorite colors for blankets she was crocheting for them. Once she started rolling she was like a machine stringing together one blanket a week, I was shocked because they were actually really good. Every time I looked around yearn was being delivered. After a while she started buying small tubs to store her yearn. A few months later she stops complaining her fingers were beginning to cramp up on her.

I know Penny, she's never going back to it so now we have about eight tubs of yearn, enough to open our own yearn outlet. It's really not a bad vision, our little outlet selling paintings, blankets, books, and now our latest item, yearn, any color you'll ever need. I would mention about her putting some money away trying to get her to understand our new norm being disabled, retired and on a fixed income but what Penny don't want to hear she won't hear. That's why God sent me, I have more patience than most making it possible to look past a lot. I don't create or join in drama I avoid it. We worked hard going through hell at times to reach this place, a place of love, joy, peace and contentment we have today.

Many were blessed to receive more than they had once the stimulus money began but not all like my wife had the mind and wisdom to us it to their advantage. That's what I discovered in me, the wisdom to finally be able to use money wisely to my advantage. All I've ever known was how to throw away money and now becoming familiar with this different side was truly an eye opening experience. I was buying all that I need but the majority was being put away.

I didn't know how long this stimulus money would continue to flow but realizing an opportunity, while it was still flowing I was going to take full advantage. I wasn't going to allow me and my family to be caught out there when the flow did cease. From the way things were going I believed somehow seniors were in for a bumpy ride on our way back to normalcy.

I knew change was on its way before the pandemic. I had explained to my wife that me with no pension and only social security to rely on, and her on permanent disability we would have to downsize to cut cost and still we would be stretched to the limit. But now things had taken a whole different turn making life even more uncertain. I hate so many suffered in the midst of this pandemic. For many this past year has become a curse but for others as sad and scary as the times were and still is could still experience blessings in the midst of this storm.

I heard my wife talking on the phone telling someone I was her rock and I thought that's funny, if you feel that confident in me why don't you listen to anything I say. I've given her advice and it's like I never heard anything. One of her girlfriends will give her the same advice and she'll come back and tell me like she was hearing it for the first time. All I do is shake my head and keep it moving. Just knowing from the beginning of the stimulus package the wise move to make, and having the wisdom and focus to follow through to the end has left my wife and I in a much better position today.

Seeing how secure I've tried to make our life she knows she can depend on me, sometimes I think a little too much. I'm not complaining because I remember not long ago when it came to important matters I was the most irresponsible person you'd ever want to deal with and had been that way most of my life. I know I keep saying it but that's because it's so true, twenty-one years ago at the age of forty-four I could have never pictured me as the person I am today. Drugs was my lifeline because I believed I couldn't enjoy life without it. I couldn't function in the real world because I didn't want anything to do with it. For many years I felt my life was fine just the way it was until the bottom fell out.

I could easily look back and be angry at myself for all the time I wasted but I've come to realize no time is wasted if you've learned something in the process. Life is a learning process, even when we don't realize it we're learning. Not until a similar situation arises and we see how differently we handle it do we notice the lesson learned from previously.

For years I remained blind to all the lessons and warnings which became an automatic response. In short I was a lost soul, I had no idea who I was therefore no idea what I was capable of. I had never felt I belonged anywhere so I lived a life of adapting to fit in wherever I could. To know someone depends on me as my wife does today back then I wouldn't have been able to handle it. I would have cracked under the pressure of being responsible for someone other than myself because even my responsibility in that area was shaky.

Penny and I have been and continue to be truly blessed. My greatest blessing is being able to see myself as a wise thinking man and to be able to use the term man in the highest regard as it refers to me. Knowing I won't leave this life just knowing an empty existence fills my spirit with satisfaction. I always have to chuckle when I hear someone on TV say in a jokingly manner, "you know God works in mysterious ways". The saying has been around so long I wonder how many actually believe it. I do.

During the pandemic not just feeling but being blessed when we knew so many were suffering not only physically but financially also made me feel somewhat guilty. Even those who were being blessed financially with no close family members afflicted by the virus, many were being affected by the confinement resulting in domestic violence and even suicide. For a while things began to reflect a science fiction movie of world disaster caused by a deadly virus. The world was in a panic and rich and poor alike were living with uncertainty.

Presently I'm feeling uncomfortable writing about being so blessed during a time when so many were and are still suffering and struggling to get their lives back to some sort of normalcy. At the same time I know God's blessings are not given to us too keep to ourselves but to be a blessing to others however and whenever we can. I'm not a very good verbal communicator but He's given me the passion and talent to communicate through my writing. It brings to mind a short memory of me as a young boy. Because of my stuttering I was afraid to talk to girls out of fear of being laughed at.

So if I liked them I'd try writing love notes to express my interest. In the end I'd still get laughed at but at least it wasn't in my face. Point being writing was my way of trying to communicate even back then. I also remember as a young boy for a short time trying to put together rhyming poems so I guess the passion for writing has always been there. However when whatever is not utilized for a long period of time it can easily get buried under huge piles of mess.

Being such an unhappy child my only wish in life was to be happy. Television being my only escape back then there were very few black actors and actresses who got the opportunity to play inspiring roles. Only portrayed as butlers, maids or chauffeurs I would watch the white family sitcoms and the love and understanding that was portrayed through their characters. It didn't matter if it was real or not I just knew that was what I wanted. I also knew a chaotic childhood would be all I'd ever know.

Although it was a television program I believed there were real loving and understanding parents creating that type of environment for their children in the real world somewhere. It had to be, I was young but I knew all parents couldn't be like these. Even before truly coming to the realization of being adopted I was made to feel unwanted as if I was a burden. After getting a clearer picture and then seeing where I ended up made me feel even more of an unwanted child. I believe I mentally shut down way back then and with nothing in my life to shine any sort of brighter view over the years I would draw more distant from reality.

Some say our childhood shouldn't have anything to do with how we live our life as adults but I believe only a person who's never been through anything would make that claim. I know for a fact that opinion is false because I've been deeply affected for years. A person unable to reach full maturity until reaching his mid-forties I would say had a serious problem stimming from his childhood. It's one thing to never be able to mature which was not the case.

I also find it hard to believe that anyone who grew up psychologically and physically abused leading to mentally and physically abusing themselves the better part of their adult years could suddenly just snap out of it and decide their ready to grow up. Not even mentioning while still in growth having someone other than you depending on you. I even see that theory as a little naïve.

I look at where I am and who I am today and still find it a mystery. I could never see past where I was and in trying to move past I'd always end up on that same familiar road. In half the time it took me to hit my rock bottom today it seems like those years never existed. I still have my health and strength and I thank God every day for still being in my right mind. To be able to discover the talents that's always been in me while still among the living and able to enjoy and appreciate them.

I remember how I use to experiment with drugs and the effects of some and how I vowed to never ever try that again. One effect was so scary afterwards I was able to clearly see how a few of my friends ended up stuck in their own minds never finding their way back. They were fine one day to barely recognizing the people they see every day the next. That's why I thank God every day, I know the life I've lived, all the chances I've taken with my life and sanity out of self-pity and ignorance. I can't see myself any other way than a miracle.

Sometime just thinking to myself and wonder maybe this could be a reward for enduring the hell I created for myself without allowing it to change or harden my heart. It sure feels like a reward or rather a display of God's pleasure.

I've made a steep mountain of bad choices throughout my life and will make more, maybe not as serious as those previously but bad choices nonetheless. It's in our nature and God takes that on account and have provided a provision on His end through His son Jesus Christ but how far we allow bad choices to override common sense depends solely on us and so do the consequences that follow.

I think about Jesse who passed on not long ago. It was a shock hearing of his untimely death. For as long as I've been married he'd been holding it together. He had his own nice apartment but he struggled with loneliness.

I found it difficult to understand how a bachelor with his own apartment didn't have someone, even someone part time until better came along but he didn't even have that. At times he also felt he was being alienated by family. For short time points he would cut himself off in attempt of trying to convince himself he didn't need anyone. When I was working for the clothing firm Jesse lived walking distance from us. He and I had started play chess together so some evenings after work he'd come by and we'd play a couple games. A month later he was showing up every evening.

After a while Penny started complaining I was spending more time with him than her. Jesse hearing the news that me being a married man, although I'm home my wife is still feeling neglected will only register as rejection towards him and he'll leave hurt. I knew he was overdoing it but I also knew how lonely he was so there were times I would even allow myself to be inconvenienced. He was struggling in a lot of areas of his life and I think the struggle and loneliness is what contributed greatly to his death.

I think about how God used Jesse to bring me to where I am today. My first shelter was so clean and comfortable if I wouldn't have gotten thrown out I could see myself staying long enough to get a job and hopefully a place to stay but unfortunately following the same pattern never rising above. I believe he's experiencing inexpressible peace right now because even through his struggles God was with him and was able to use him to affect another's life in a way he never could imagine.

God is well aware that many of us in our life-time will need supernatural intervention to guide us out of the hell we face or the one we've created for ourselves right here on earth. He understands our sinful nature along with the inner and outward struggles we face daily and is always ready, willing and able to keep or to set us back on course. When I first read Romans 8:15-17 where Paul describes his inner struggles I undeniably could relate to what he was experiencing.

Paul wrote: ***For what I am doing I do not understand, for I am not practicing what I would like to do but I am doing the very things I hate. But if I do the very thing I do not want to do I agree with the law, confessing that the law is good. So now, no*** *longer am I the one doing it, but sin which dwells in me. For I know that nothing good dwells in me, that is in my flesh. For the willing is present in me but the doing of the good is not.* Paul's confession hit me like a brick. He was describing my struggle to the letter. I had suffered many years and no matter how deep my desire, how many promises I made to myself all my attempts toward change failed and I never could understand why.

If a person truly wanted change for him or herself why would it seem so impossible to achieve? It's one thing working and wanting to change someone else but if the change is focused on self-improvement why must it be such a struggle for so many. I asked myself that question over and over, why was it so hard getting control of my own life. The word of God revealed I was in control, in fact that's how I ended up where I was, being in control. Instead of listening to wise counsel when I had the chance I chose to follow unwise counsel. Over time I became so lost to my own identity I couldn't find my way back without the proper guidance.

Sitting here writing this book, I could have never foreseen me doing this. The most famous fortune teller in the world whoever that is wouldn't have been able to convince me that one day I would even be capable of doing this. Me, a person who didn't achieve a GED until he was in his mid-forties, whose life was a continuous thirty plus years of jumping from one drug to another. A person who felt he had nothing to offer the world, not even good memories as a tribute to his own life.

God seen in me what I couldn't see in myself and because He was able to get through to me He was able to repair and prepare me to be a blessing to someone else. That's what He does, He saves that we may proclaim our life saving experience with others that they may search to reach their own experience with Him.

God is never hard to find because He's always there, we're the ones who walk away choosing to do our own thing because the things of the world seems more realistic to us. Things we can see, feel and taste are natural but when speaking of beyond this world but also connected to this world able to affect our very being in the most extraordinary ways, it sounds unbelievable. Because it sounds so unreal many refuse to accept any other view, it sounds unreal so it must be. If not backed by some scientific fact it's not believable and that's cool. We all have to live our own life believing what we choose to believe. If you've always rejected God's existence you've never had an experience with him, so it's easy to reject what you've never been able to experience yourself.

We see, hear and experience so much in the world that discredits the existence of God and it's truly unfortunate. Because of hypocrites, those who call themselves children of God but think and live like the devil. Because of false preachers and teachers who profit off blind believers who don't know the word of God for themselves. There are a number of reason but the two I've listed bother me the most. That's why we need to read God's word to know him for ourselves and not just go by what we've heard from the preacher. His written word is able to being understanding to our own lives by reading and allowing his word to speak and teach our spirit.

Here's something to wrap your brain around. Who has more free time for reading than inmates? We've heard one time or other on the news or maybe a prison documentary of inmates finding God while in prison. A place where a hardened heart is a requirement for daily survival. A peace where kindness and compassion can easily be perceived as weakness making yourself a target. We heard their confessed religious transformation and thought, oh ya, now you find God after you've gotten caught and facing the consequences of your actions.

But if you think about it, it's not as if they get any prison brownie points for changing their view, so why the change? It's not like joining some prison religion because strength in number means protection, when's the last time you heard of a Christian prison gang. So if there's no true benefits in it for them, then why? Many being interviewed said they found peace in God's word.

Think about it, is there any other book you've ever heard of that's able to produce a peace you didn't have but now have while still in the midst of your hell. Is there any other book in which millions over the years, all over the world have confessed have changed their lives in the most amazing ways. There's millions of books and almost as many religions in the world but the bible, the written word of God's has stood the test of time even after numerous attempts over the centuries to discredit its authenticity, why is that?

It's because the bible is not just a book of empty words. Going back to ***Hebrews 4:12: For the word of God is alive and active and sharper than any two-edged sword and piercing as far as the division of soul and spirit, of both joints and marrow, and able to judge the thoughts and intentions of the heart.*** In other words the word of God cuts through to the root of our problems. Man works from the outside in treating the symptoms but God works from the inside out attacking the cause.

I've come to believe for myself in the supernatural properties attached to God's word because He is his word able to do what it says He can and does do in the lives of all those who come to Him with open an willing hearts. The beautiful thing is it doesn't matter who or where we are. I among millions are in what could be the scariest stage of a person's life, senior life. Especially a person who knows he or she hasn't always done the right things to prepare for this time. Whose now sole income relies on what the government is willing to give for the years of contributions.

It can make a person who has always held his or her own to now suddenly feel like a dependent. As I wrote earlier, I believed based on our retired income it would require some real unwanted changes and I'm not talking of a temporary situation, this was for the rest of our life.

Today I have a more comfortable outlook on our time ahead. I've wasted thousands of dollars over the years, a few times having enough in lump sums to start over but wasted it all without a second thought.

Blessed with one more opportunity this was the very first time I followed wisdom instead of stupidity and the results have been outstanding. During the pandemic we didn't receive any more than what most Americans received but the results of following wisdom made it seem as though we was. **Psalms 111:10 says the fear of the Lord is the beginning of wisdom.** The term fear relates to reverence or respect for who God is. The wisdom that God gives is able to take us well beyond our own expectations.

I heard it said that you don't meet God until you've truly been through something, something too much for us to deal with. That's when we usually seek God the hardest, in the midst of a terrible storm. **Proverbs 8:17 God says, I love those who love me; and those who diligently seek me will find me.** God doesn't turn anyone away, it may seem that way but it's not his will that we go through any of this mess. He created the world but we created the mess.

He could have created human beings to be by nature obedient without question but where's the growth in that? God created us to grow and learn moving towards developing into the best vision of ourselves. Created with free-will to make our own choices good or bad gives us that freedom to do what God intended. However most times we choose to do things our way instead of God's way because we like shortcuts and God doesn't do shortcuts. We want to grow up before our time because we crave our inde- pendence, we crave freedom to make our own deci- sions without the willingness to take direction or correction.

Without the wisdom to make wise choices we find ourselves living a life of making bad choices and many times the same bad choice over and over. Today the world is in the condition it's in because of the bad choices that's been made over the years through lack of spiritual or inner growth which pro- duces sound wisdom.

God knows our inner as well as outward strug- gles and deeply desires to be involved but He won't invade anyone's life because that interferes with free-will so He waits patiently for an invitation. Many times the invitation won't come for years after we've dug a hole so deep for ourselves we can't climb out.

He's also saddened by those He will never receive an invitation from because of their stubbornness, their fixed mindset of rejecting the belief of God's existence and ability to effect lives today. The bible tells us that many will be called but few will hear. If you refuse Him he has no choice but to refuse you, how can you be a friend to someone who wants nothing to do with you.

The peace and joy I've found, the goodness and wonders I've experienced, and the love I feel from within teaches me how to be a more loving person. Twenty-one years ago after thirty-five years of mad- ness I could have never pictured myself existing in such peace, joy and contentment. Life is better today than it's ever been and I know it didn't come to pass through my own strength or intelligence. God not only hears our outward but our inner silent cries and jumps at the chance to respond but many times His timing doesn't coincide with ours and we quickly reach the conclusion He doesn't hear, He's doesn't care, or He's not there.

We need what we need and we need it now is how the world operates but God doesn't operate in our time and space. In *Isaiah 55:8-9* God says: *For My thought are not your thoughts, neither are your ways My ways declares the Lord. For as the heavens are higher than the earth, so are My ways higher than your ways and My thoughts than your thoughts.* God doesn't give anything unless we're prepared to receive it. Would you give keys to a car to your young teenager without a license and not knowing the first thing about driving, I should hope not knowing it could end in disaster.

That teenager won't get all he or she needs to drive a car in one day, not ever one month and a month of anticipation to a young teen could feel like six months. If the teen wants the keys he or she must give into patience while doing what is needed in order to receive the keys and the car. God operates by the same principle, He won't give us anything unless He knows we're prepared in every way to handle it knowing it could end in disaster otherwise. He will always give us his best which most times turns out to be more than we expected and more than expected to an unprepared mind is a recipe for disaster.

God is in the business of restoring lives and relationships. My one regret which I thought would never be resolved was the relationship I could never have with my son. In the beginning although twenty-one I was still too immature to fully understand my responsibilities. Later in life as drugs began becoming a big part of my existence I found myself in a dysfunctional state of mind, a deterioration of my common sense. When Jerome was born in 1977 as I said I was twenty-one and his mother was in her early or mid-thirties. One mid-summer afternoon I was hanging out with one of my biological sisters. Following her into a bar Kitty and her sister were there having drinks. My sister introduced us and Kitty immediately started showing interest.

Seeing her reaction and always having an attraction for older women the hormones began kicking in. I always seen myself as an improviser, I still wasn't much of a talker but I'd become pretty good at playing the shy role to my advantage seeing how they seemed to enjoy unwrapping the mystery. Kitty already having three kids the last thing on my mind was her getting or even wanting to be pregnant. When she hit me with the news of her pregnancy I was caught completely off guard.

My first feeling about the news was doubt that it was mine for two reasons. First we hadn't even known each other a good four months yet and second, when we met she was living with a guy, in fact me and friends of mine helped her move. As far as I knew she might have already been pregnant at that point, so as you can see my doubt was justified.

About a month after getting the news I received a letter requesting me to appear in family court. I'm nervous now because I have no idea what this letter is about but Kitty's name is also mentioned in the letter.

I asked her about it but came away still with no idea what was going on. I didn't know anything about welfare, what was that and what did it have to do with me? Once I got in court the judge was nice enough to clear it all up for me. Able to see the age difference the judge looking at us ask me a couple times if I was sure the baby was mine. For some reason even through the doubt each time he asked I said yes.

Still not comprehending the seriousness of the situation I went on with life as usual. Even being there in the hospital when Jerome was born and the one to name him didn't motivated any type of change in my mentality. I remained blind to the reality that I was now responsible for another life, I didn't know what it meant or detailed. In fact I left the courthouse believing the payments the judge had ordered me to pay each week until the child was eighteen was the sum of my responsibility. I would show up from time to time not really knowing what I should do or say. I took him to the park a few times but I think mostly that was to show him off, he was a cute little fella.

Other than buying him a pair sneakers when he was about six years old I wasn't much of a dad. Not that I didn't want to be, I didn't know how to be.

Months later she moved out of town without a word and I lost touch all together. I tried going online in search of him by his and her name but really had no idea what I was doing, I was just feeling my way but getting nowhere, so that was a waste. As the years pasted I would frequently think about him, how he was doing, if he was ok. The only child I had fathered I knew I had missed out on a part of life I would never again get to experience, being a dad.

As the years continued to pass I began feeling it may be too late, too many years between us. I'd imagine the worst scenario of his response towards me as he pointed out how I wasn't there when he needed a father, so why show up now. What answer could I give that would curve the anger or maybe even hatred he may feel towards me. Even the thought that maybe it would be better to leave things as is crossed my mind. Being over thirty years maybe it was a selfish attempt to ease my guilt. As far as I knew he was married with a family of his own, what need did he have for a father now?

About three or four months after those two slick detectives came to the house and deprived me of my pork-chop sandwich still caught up, a bunch of us crack smokers were in the house getting high and suddenly there was a knock on the door. Joyce's son answered the door, then turned and said it was for me which was odd because I rarely had visitors.

When I got to the door a young female I'd never seen was standing there with a baby carriage. Standing in the doorway high and now confused she began telling me my son was locked up in the same county jail I was recently released from and wanted me to visit him. She also had a letter he mailed to her to pass on which told how he had be searching awhile for me. Find out, he went on a website anyone can access which confirms whether or not a person has a criminal record, and that's how he found me, now ain't that a, you know what. Don't worry, God enjoys humor, why you think He made funny people?

From that website he was able to find me and my current address. For over seventeen years I had no idea where he was, I would have never thought to look there. Suddenly, out of the blue I find out he's walking distance away. It was a joyful but troubling moment at the same time. My son actually found and wanted to see me but to also hear the news of him being locked up was troubling to say the least because he had no business being there. I automatically felt the need to share the blame feeling that maybe if I could have been there this route may have been avoided.

When the young mother showed up she was on her way for a visit then and asked if I wanted to accompany her but I wasn't about to go up in there in my condition. The atmosphere alone would have made me too paranoid. I can just see me standing there in line waiting to get in all sweaty and fidgety trying not to display that guilty look. Go in for a visit and end up an inmate, no thank you. Good thing it was against regulations for former inmates to visit until six months after their release date because it gave me the perfect excuse.

The sad truth which I need to confess is that at the time she mentioned accompanying her I had reservations about leaving. A party was going on behind me and my best friend at that time was there calling me to hurry back while it was still there to take me where I wanted to be. So at that point we didn't get to reconnect with each other. It was about a year later when we finally did reconnect. Anticipation and excitement was felt by both of us.

I remember just before going into the Mission Joyce had told me Jerome had come there looking for me but didn't leave any contact information. Close to a year later Penny and I had recently gotten married. Setting back one evening watching TV Penny came rushing towards me like a kid full of surprise with phone in, the next words I heard were "your son is on the phone". I was like, what? And she said it gain. I almost couldn't believe it, he was like a private eye, how did find me this time, how'd he get this number? I was so glad he did but if he would have been someone out to arrest me I'd be in serious trouble with him on the case. I had no idea how to find him and he found me twice seemingly with little effort.

We talked by phone a few times before meeting. At the time he was living in upstate New York with his then girlfriend and her kids including their twin daughters, Avaya and Alivia. When we finally got together at our home he also brought his girlfriend and two daughters with him and what a glorious occasion it was. I not only had my son but two granddaughters and in addition are two other grands I haven't met yet. Today my son and I have a great relationship and life has blossomed for us both with a bitter sweet mix.

Months after our first reunion the mother of the twins suffered a stroke which left her permanently unresponsive. Meanwhile the court had awarded temporary custody of the kids to a close friend of the mother. Jerome's life now coming together with marriage in the plans to a beautiful strong woman he reconnected with, backing him together they began proceedings for full custody of the twins.

In early 2021 he was awarded full custody and now resides in Maryland with his fiancée, her son who is off to college, and two eight years old twin girls. They've had their first sleep over which was interesting and fun. We talk by phone regularly, the girls even call us on their little phones. Just to hear them call grandma and grandpa is like sweet music to our ears. Penny having two daughters but also believing she would never be a grandmother is more thrilled than I am. To hear grandma and know they're not just the kids from the neighborhood you adopted gives you a whole different feeling.

I couldn't undo or redo what already was but God has brought me full circle, I can't be the dad I should have been back then but there's still room for me to be a father and with an added bonus, I get to be a granddad. As I said God not only restores lives, He can also restore families in way we'd never imagine. Yes, He truly works in mysterious ways and

I'm enjoying seeing His work applied in my life. I'm one of many who believe there are no coincidences in this life, nor things just happening by chance. I believe God has a designed plan for each one of us, designed according to our personality and gifts.

However He doesn't demand we take or even stay on that path. Already knowing who will as well as won't receive Him still He chose to leave the choosing up to us and that's where most of us get into trouble. God allows us to choose because God wants us to desire Him of our own free-will but we desire to test the waters first and many get washed away by the worldly desires we contract along the way. Thank God for never giving up on us even when friends and love ones give up, even when we give up on ourselves He knows the day and the hour of our return and meanwhile waits patiently.

All I had lost along the way, hope, peace, joy, contentment, direction, purpose and family, all these attributes and more have been added or restored to me and not by my own power, smarts or ingenuity. By the Power of God through Jesus Christ. He heard my cries and felt my pain and at the proper time came to my recue. For some it sounds hard to believe, some might even say I'm fooling myself refusing to believe what sounds impossible. Yes, to unbelievers it does sound impossible, even though I experienced supernatural intervention in my life it still seems impossible but undeniably here I am.

Today I'm able to see that He had to wait until I was truly ready and that time would only come when I ran out of options, when I had nowhere else to run.

I had to reach that point to enable me to see where I was, and only then would I come to my senses realizing how lost I was. Realizing your lost is one thing, finding your way back is something completely different. If you don't know how you got where you are in the first place without proper guidence chances are you'll remain lost.

On that cold winter night and day with no warm place to stay or lay my head I felt as lost as ever. I hadn't faced anything like this or felt this alone since I was a kid running away from home in winter. The difference is then I had a choice, here I didn't, I was stuck with no idea what to do. For me to say that after thirty plus years I finally got so fed up that suddenly a light just clicked on and I decided right then and there I would straighten out my life would be a lie. What I experienced could never be denied and I'd be afraid to try to, the Lord giveth and the Lord can taketh away, why take the chance.

What more can I say without quoting a bunch of biblical scriptures. I will tell you the first book of the bible we studied in the Mission which opened my eyes to so much, it was The Gospel According to John. God desires that those who don't but desire to know Him to open His word and learn of Him for yourself. I remember my amazing experience, while reading and discussing John's writings it felt as if the scriptures were speaking directly to my circumstance as if the bible knew me. The more I learned the more I wanted to know. We were fortunate to attend bible studies taught by ministers and pastors who knew from experience what it was to be lost. They were able to teach in a way that allied God's word with our present day circumstances.

I have a great deal of respect for pastors and ministers who aren't afraid of who they use to be, we all have a past. Many work so hard wanting to be held in such high regards by all they forget God gave us all our greatest tool towards encouraging others, our testimony. I'll never be ashamed of who I was, without that person I wouldn't be who I am today. I use to say if only I knew then what I know now.

Maybe I'd be richer and certainly wiser but there's ups and downs whichever way we go and it's a proven fact that the higher the level the bigger the devil. So there always the possibility of a downfall but now on a larger scale, taking all that into account, I think I'm where and who I 'm supposed to be.

I hope this book has in some way, shape, or form has been enlightening and a joy to read because I enjoyed writing it. The first version has always been close to my heart because it was something I was led to, not something planned. When the concept entered my mind I was automatically willing to go with it. The more it evolved the more I saw this work as a necessary part of my healing process. Memories playing a big part in who we are too become. They are silent echoes from our past only we hear. They echo the good as well as the bad but what happens when the bad heavily outweigh the good, it can create unstable individuals. I was never a threat to others but I was thoughtless when it came to my own wellbeing.

Seeing all that was being released and feeling the weight being lifted I could feel a light overwhelming the shadows that overshadowed my existence. However in the process realizing the direction I was headed I found myself getting anxious to speed things up. I couldn't believe or wait to see my published book with my name on it as the author. I was quickly forgetting I was led and because I moved ahead of God's timing I found myself unsatisfied with the results. After fifteen years I had almost given up hope of getting another chance but here we are.

A work inspired by God, if He wasn't satisfied He wasn't going to allow me to be either. I'd get another chance but at His time on His terms, the two things I lacked, patience and focus is a most. Why so long you may ask? Within those fifteen years there were two other books published I rarely mention because I consider them lessons to be learned. As you can see I still hadn't learned much. Because I was now a published author I had this, well that's what I told myself anyway.

As I look back now all I see is wasted time and money. The lesson learned, if God leads us to it He'll guide us through it, and apart from Him it may still come to pass but without the added benefits He provides. God has brought me full circle to experience a more fulfilling life. Today I'm at peace with myself as well as the life I live. I never thought I'd experience witnessing my life meaning so much too so many, all because of the person I am today. I've always wanted to go on a cruise but for one thing it was always too expensive.

Also it just doesn't seem like something a person does by his or herself. I can't even get Penny to get in a canoe where we're close to land, a ship out in the middle of the ocean with no land in sight, I think not. I might as well have said I'm taking you to the dentist to get your two aching teeth pulled, I'd get the same response. In August one of Rhonda's daughters, my niece planned a family seven day cruise which falls on my sixty-six birthday. When Rhonda called asking if I was interested I jumped at the opportunity without even thinking about the cost. Not long ago I wouldn't have been able to afford to even think about it.

To be offered this opportunity at this particular time leaving port on my birthday making it undoubtedly the best birthday I've ever had is nothing short of God's blessing on my life. I get to fulfill a desire I've had since the original love boat series but unfortunately Penny won't be accompanying me but I'm sure she won't get bored. I figure being partners she saved me money on the cruise and not taking that into consideration and not sharing in the blessing is not God's desire nor mine. So contributing to the fight against boredom is a small price to pay for enjoying the best birthday ever.

As I writing this book all arrangements have been finalized but the cruise date hasn't approached yet. However I felt the need to share this to show God gives the desires of our hearts as long as it lines up with His will. God's will is that we live a loving and fulfilling life and knowing us better than we know ourselves He won't give what He knows we're not prepared to handle. God is in the business of building up, if we got what we wanted when we wanted it most would end up self-destructing sooner than later never getting the chance to meet and know Him.

Remember I met Him on a dark freezing winter evening after over three decades of madness, imagine before then getting everything I wanted when I wanted it, I probably wouldn't have lasted one decade let alone three. God is real and His word is true and on that I stake my life. Because of Him I have life and life more abundantly. Today I'm able to see over the horizon while moving forward instead of continuing to be led by what's behind.

The best news I know to give is that what I have is not exclusive, in fact the sign outside the door reads, "Come one come all, open 24/7". What I found in my journey towards self-discovery is that I'm a child of God made in His image and likeness to be a victor in life and not a victim, to be a blessing and not a curse. He didn't save me because I deserved it but because I needed it. Know that God is always in the midst just waiting for your invitation

A part of me absorbed within the pages of this book has enjoyed the time we spent together and I pray you be lifted up by God's love and covered in His righteousness. I pray that you keep the faith because we walk be faith, not by sight.

God Bless.

Dedication

I dedicate this book to my biological mother Jessie Lue Kearney, although she didn't raise me the time we shared in later years I truly enjoyed and cherish. Seeing how much of me came from her, a compassionate heart, a warm disposition, sense of humor, and always wearing a smile in spite of circumstances. Over the years as we grew closer she'd refer to me as her twin because of the strong resemblance. As it became more public those who knew my mother would tell me how much I look like her. I'll miss her smile and radiating love I felt every time she saw me approaching. I know without a doubt she's in a much better place, I love you mom.

CPSIA information can be obtained
at www.ICGtesting.com
Printed in the USA
LVHW071647210122
709067LV00020B/694